1848:
THE REVOLUTION OF
THE INTELLECTUALS

1848:
THE REVOLUTION OF
THE INTELLECTUALS

by
SIR LEWIS NAMIER
Late Fellow of the Academy

With a new Introduction by
JAMES JOLL
Fellow of the Academy

Published for THE BRITISH ACADEMY
by OXFORD UNIVERSITY PRESS

Oxford University Press, Walton Street, Oxford OX2 6DP

Oxford New York Toronto
Delhi Bombay Calcutta Madras Karachi
Petaling Jaya Singapore Hong Kong Tokyo
Nairobi Dar es Salaam Cape Town
Melbourne Auckland

and associated companies in
Berlin Ibadan

Oxford is a trade mark of Oxford University Press

Published in the United States
by Oxford University Press, New York

Lecture © The Master and Fellows of Balliol College Oxford 1946
Introduction © The British Academy 1992

Reprinted from Proceedings of the British Academy, Volume XXX
First published 1946
6th impression 1971
New paperback edition 1992
Reprinted 1993

ISBN 0–19–726111–6

Printed and bound in Great Britain by
Biddles Ltd, Guildford and King's Lynn

INTRODUCTION

by
JAMES JOLL

I N 1957, three years before his death, Sir Lewis Namier wrote: 'For forty years I have wanted to write a history of Europe 1812–1914, and I studied various aspects of it in days when Europe was still supreme in the world. But circumstances were against the scheme, and the best years I had for historical research were taken up by work on British Parliamentary history and on pre-1939 diplomacy; and now at the age of nearly seventy, I see the rest of my life under a heavy mortgage to the *History of Parliament*, and to further work on materials I have been collecting for it most of my life. With the darkness of old age rapidly advancing, I can hardly hope to return to my other pet scheme.'[1] What remains of this 'other pet scheme' is a number of volumes of essays, some unpublished drafts and this short but substantial volume, *1848: The Revolution of the Intellectuals*, an expanded version of Namier's Raleigh Lecture to the British Academy, delivered in 1944.

The tension between Namier's commitment to British parliamentary history and his commitment to — indeed involvement in — modern European history is a typical aspect of a life full of contradictions. Namier was, as Sir Isaiah Berlin has suggested, someone who combined a deep natural romanticism with a historical method that was essentially empiricist and positivistic.[2] He was by birth, upbringing and early experience a product of the tensions and problems of Central Europe. He was born in 1888, the son of a prosperous Jewish landowner in Austrian Poland who had converted to Catholicism, and Namier never lost both his sense of involvement in the fate of the Habsburg Monarchy and its successor states and of European Jewry. He rejected his parents' attempt at assimilation into Austrian society and reverted to Judaism, and he was later to play a considerable role in the Zionist movement. But it was his

[1] Sir Lewis Namier, *Vanished Supremacies* (pbk edn, Harmondsworth, 1962), p.7.
[2] Isaiah Berlin, 'L. B. Namier', *Personal Impressions* (London, 1980), pp.63-82.

education in England — especially at Balliol — that filled him
with a romantic feeling for what he saw as the stability of England
and its conservative institutions, and with admiration for the
British landed aristocracy and gentry whose members were to be
the main subject of his two major works on 18th-century political
history, *The Structure of Politics at the Accession of George III* and
England in the Age of the American Revolution. Yet for all his
enthusiasm for Zionism and his immersion in the lives and
archives of the British upper classes, and in spite of a very active
professional life and a growing reputation as a historian, he
remained an unhappy man, suffering from a sense of alienation
and very sensitive to the fact that his scholarly achievements had
not led to total recognition and acceptance. Only a late second
marriage (and a conversion to Anglicanism which lost him some
of his Zionist friends) brought him a measure of tranquillity at the
end of his life. In 1931 he was appointed Professor of History at
Manchester University, a post he held until 1953, but which, it
must be admitted, he probably regarded as only second best in
comparison with more prestigious chairs at Oxford and
Cambridge to which he was rightly entitled as a scholar, but which
he never obtained — partly undoubtedly because of his difficult
personality. In Sir Isaiah Berlin's words, 'Those who met him
were divided into some who looked on him as a man of genius and
a dazzling talker and others who fled from him as an appalling
bore . . . Academics and civil servants, whom he bullied, loathed
and denigrated him. Scholars looked on him as a man of
prodigious powers and treated him with deep, if at times
somewhat nervous admiration.'[3]

Namier became a British citizen in 1913 and during the First
World War worked for the political intelligence department of
the Foreign Office and became deeply involved in Polish affairs,
so much so that the Polish statesman Roman Dmowski, with
whose policies Namier disagreed and to whom he attributes in a
footnote in this book 'the meanness of Fascism', tried to get him
fired and disgraced, or even, as Namier apparently believed, to
have him assassinated. Namier's dislike of Austria-Hungary and
his delight at its disintegration in 1918 was matched by an even
greater dislike of the Germans, a dislike that was to grow to hatred
under the impact of events of the 1930s and 40s. In the meantime,
Namier had gone into business and had raised enough money
from this and other sources to devote himself to historical
research: the result was his two books on 18th-century politics: *The*

[3] Berlin, op. cit., p.70.

Structure of Politics at the Accession of George III appeared in 1929 and *England in the Age of the American Revolution* a year later. These works, even if the latter does not quite live up to the promise of its title, established the author as an original and formidable scholar whose detailed reconstruction of the background of the members of parliament, the working of the unreformed electoral system in the constituencies and of the network of patronage enabled him to demolish many of the accepted views of the nature of political parties and the role of King George III, so that he introduced a new dimension into the study of the English 18th century. But it was characteristic of Namier that his rigorous scholarship and his endless research in local record offices and the archives of country houses should have been accompanied by less orthodox methods — the consultation of a graphologist to analyse the character of the author of a manuscript and a firm belief in Freudian psychoanalysis.

Although all his later life Namier worked on his studies of the British parliament and political system in the 18th century, he was also deeply and practically involved in Zionist politics (an aspect of his life studied in Norman Rose's *Lewis Namier and Zionism* [Oxford, 1980]), and he was a polemical student of international relations and a fierce reviewer, so that his volumes of essays and his study of the origins of the Second World War *Diplomatic Prelude 1938–1939* (London, 1948) form a substantial part of his *oeuvre*, even if they have sometimes been severely judged. As Linda Colley writes in her perceptive study of his work, 'Few great historians have been more clever or more obsessively hardworking than Namier, but fewer still have produced so little durable work or so much that was uneven in quality.'[4] It is a harsh judgment, because the vigour of Namier's prose, his uncompromisingly independent views and his extraordinary mastery of the sources all make even his slighter reviews and essays still worth reading.

By the 1940s Namier was reflecting more and more on the course of German history, remarking in 1947 that 'the century which has closed is that of German predominance in Europe, the age which has closed is that of European predominance in the world.'[5] Two practical incentives to work on a key episode in modern German history presented themselves in the late 1940s:

[4] Linda Colley, *Namier* (London, 1989), p.3.
[5] Colley, op. cit., p.14, quoting from unpublished notes for Namier's Waynflete Lectures.

in 1943 the British Academy invited Namier to deliver the Raleigh Lecture on History for 1944, and in 1947 Namier gave the Waynflete Lectures at Magdalen College, Oxford on the Frankfort parliament of 1848 — a brilliant attempt, still vivid in the minds of those who heard the lectures, to apply the methods Namier had used in the study of the 18th century English parliament to the very different circumstances of Germany in the mid-19th century. Thus in fact for several years Namier was applying his penetrating intellect and powers of research to a study of the revolutions of 1848 especially in Germany and Austria. The present lecture, expanded fourfold from the version actually delivered, is an important and still valuable result.

Originally Namier wanted to call his lecture simply '1848', writing to the President of the British Academy that 'It is after all as significant a date as 1066.' And although he later indicated the direction in which his analysis was to point by adding the sub-title 'The Revolution of the Intellectuals', he was in fact demonstrating that 1848, for all the apparent failure of the individual revolutions of that year, was, as he put it, 'a seed plot of history.' 'The basic conflict of 1848,' he wrote, 'was between two principles — of dynastic property in countries, and of national sovereignty: the one feudal in origin, historic in its growth and survival, deeply rooted but difficult to defend in argument; the other grounded in reason and ideas, simple and convincing, but as unsuited to living organisms as chemically pure water.' (p.25) The result was that 1848 inaugurated a new age, not of liberalism as many of the revolutionaries hoped, but of a nationalism that was to destroy liberal constitutionalism: 'Acid nationalisms based on language (on plenty of it and little in it) originate mainly with urban middle-class intellectuals; and this is why 1848 is of such supreme importance in the growth of European nationalisms.' (p.101)

It is on central and eastern Europe, on Germany's eastern borders and on the territories of the Habsburg Empire that Namier concentrates. And one can perhaps see how exciting he found his theme because of the regret he felt, in spite of ranging very widely, at having to leave out so much: 'An analysis of other problems in 1848 — those of German unity, of the Habsburg Monarchy, of the Hungarian National State, of the "subject nationalities", of Italy, of parliamentary assemblies, etc., I must leave for further essays.' (p.33) The book ends with yet another unfulfilled promise: after a long quotation from Herzen likening the German revolution to a cow — 'that excellent and respected animal' — gambolling and galloping in a meadow, Namier writes 'But the domestic story of the German revolution — that playful cow — I must leave to another essay.' (p.124)

But while regretting that Namier never fully explored all the paths he opens up, we must be grateful for what we have — over a hundred pages of brilliant comment and erudite information based on a characteristically thorough grasp of the sources (though we are also reminded of the limitations on research in European history imposed by the Second World War: in several footnotes Namier points out that some of the foreign works he would have liked to consult were not available in the British Museum). Namier had an innate understanding of central Europe and he had a formidable command of languages: it is salutary to find the remark appended to his recommendation of a work on the Slav renaissance, 'The book is in Croat.'

Although there are interesting comments on the international relations of 1848 and an excellent analysis of the ambiguities in the relationship between Prussia and Russia, as well as an account of French foreign policy under Lamartine which gives the poet more credit as a statesman than he is usually allowed by historians, the central parts of the work are those which deal with Poland and the relations of the Frankfort and Vienna parliaments with the Slavs. For all his criticism of the lack of realism of the Polish leaders, the aristocrats and gentry who 'dreamt of a national revolution and war, and figured a system of world politics pivoting on Poland, gyrating round her, consummated in her resurrection and culminating in her renewed greatness,' (p.14) Namier realized the tragedy of the Polish situation. Support for the Polish cause was part of every liberal programme; but when it came to practical action, that support very easily turned to betrayal. It is in discussing the Polish question that Namier's hatred of the Germans emerges most clearly — and reminds us that, for all its lasting value, the book was written during a war which to Namier seemed due to German national attitudes already expressed in 1848. For example, a democratic member of the Frankfort national assembly, Wilhelm Jordan, dismissed a proposal to grant some self-government to the predominantly Polish part of the Prussian province of Posen (Posnan) with the words: 'Are half a million Germans to live under a German government and form part of the great German Federation, or are they to be relegated to the inferior position of naturalised foreigners subject to a nation of lesser cultural content than themselves . . . ?' (p.88) One can see that such language seemed to Namier to be very similar to Hitler's complaints about the fate of the Germans in the Polish Corridor in 1939. Jordan's speech went on to state that 'Mere existence does not entitle a people to political independence: only the force to assert itself a State among others.' This summarized the whole concept of *Realpolitik* as Bismarck was to practice it. But it also foreshadows many of the key ideas of late 19th- and 20th-century nationalism: the Rankean idea that what determines a state's development is its ability to hold its own among other states; and, more ominously, the idea, shared by Marx and Engels as well as by many German liberals, that some nations are inherently superior to others, so that the inferior nations have no choice except absorption or obliteration.

For Namier the real revolution of 1848 was over before it began. In his view, the workers and peasants started the revolution, but they soon lost interest, leaving the revolution to be continued by the middle class. 'The working classes touched off,' he writes of the February Revolution in Paris, 'and the middle classes cashed in on it.' (p.7) Working class demands for social reform were crushed or ignored by a middle class increasingly terrified of mob violence. As for the peasants, once the feudal burdens under which they still laboured had been abolished they lost any desire to revolt. 'When on 7 September [1848] the Emancipation Act passed its last reading [in the Vienna parliament] the peasant masses lost further interest in Parliament; and it did not revive even when reaction swept away most of the work of the revolution, for the agrarian settlement remained untouched.' And Namier summed up his thesis as follows: 'The proletariate was defeated in Paris, the peasants were bought off in the Habsburg Monarchy. The social forces behind the revolution of 1848, disjointed and insufficient from the very outset, were thus practically eliminated. What remained was the middle classes led by intellectuals, and their modern ideology with which they confronted the old established powers and interests.' (pp.23–4).

Reading *The Revolution of the Intellectuals* some fifty years after it was written, one is struck by the power of Namier's mind as well as by the strength of his prejudices and the passion that underlies his historical writing. This lecture gave him the occasion to express some of his deepest feelings — his contempt for liberal intellectuals, his longing for a stable social order, his dislike of humbug and sloppy thinking. Although in the decades since he

wrote, historians' interest has focussed on other problems of the
revolutions of 1848 — among them the complexity of notions
such as 'working class' and 'middle class', the beginnings of
political organisation on the Right in Germany, the process of
'modernization' — the main themes discussed by Namier seem
even more relevant than they did at the time of the delivery of the
Raleigh Lecture. For all his dislike of enquiries which would, as he
put it in his Creighton Lecture in the University of London in
1952 'take us into inscrutable depths or an airy void,'[6] Namier's
concern is to bring out some of the deeper trends in the 19th and
20th centuries. And although he was sceptical about the role of
ideas in history, it is in fact with the influence of the idea of
nationalism that he is dealing — 'the passionate creed of the
intellectuals [which] invades the politics of central and east-central
Europe, and with 1848 starts the Great European War of every
nation against its neighbours.' (p.33) One of the tragic aspects of
1848 is the way in which an initial belief that constitutional
government would automatically lead to international harmony,
and that, just as in a liberal state it was hoped that conflicts of
interest between individuals and social groups could be solved by
a rational compromise, so national groups could also co-operate
for the benefit of all, turned out to be an illusion. It is this illusion
that Namier sets out to expose: 'The sovereignty of the people
merely substitutes the proprietary claims of nations for those of
princes, because States are still based on territories and not on
"sovereign" hordes; and the conflicts grow fiercer.' (p.27)

Namier believed that the old pre-revolutionary order, before
the sovereignty of princes was replaced by the 'sovereignty of the
people', at least provided a stability that was being increasingly
lost during the hundred years after 1848. 'In the interplay
between constitutional and national movements on the European
Continent, which opens in 1848,' he writes, 'it is the latter that win:
and they cut across into the international arena. A constitutional
regime is secure when its ways have become engrained in the
habits and instinctive reactions — dans les moeurs — of the political
nation: it safeguards civilized life, but it presupposes agreement
and stability as much as it secures them; and it can hardly be
expected to build up, recast, or dissect the body in which it
resides. (Hence the talk about "missed opportunities" of uniting
Germany by "Parliamentary action" lacks substance.) States are
not created or destroyed, and frontiers redrawn or obliterated, by

6 Namier,'Basic Factors in Nineteenth Century European History', *Personalities
and Power* (London, 1955), p.105.

frontiers redrawn or obliterated, by argument and majority votes; nations are freed, united, or broken by blood and iron and not by a generous application of liberty and tomato sauce; violence is the instrument of national movements.' (p.31) For Namier the only constitutional system that will work is one like that in England for which he had a Burkean admiration. And if a nation is not fortunate enough to possess that continuing heritage, then its government is best left in the hands of traditional dynasties and hierarchies. Namier's immersion in the workings of the British constitution in the 18th century colours his judgment of the liberal hopes of 1848.

Some of the events of 1848 and the lessons Namier draws from them seem oddly familiar in the 1990s when the collapse of Communist regimes in eastern Europe is accompanied by revived nationalist feuds, between, for example, Czechs and Slovaks or between Serbs and Croats. This suggests that the overthrow of a tyrannical system and a transition to some form of democracy does not mean that national passions will diminish and that national groups, on breaking free from the uniformity imposed by a dictatorshop, will necessarily learn to live at peace with each other. The processes analysed by Namier are at work even more strongly than in 1848, and I suspect that Namier with his powerful and pessimistic imagination might have felt a certain satisfaction that his diagnosis is still applicable.

In 1944 Namier was probably in a minority in being glad that the revolution of 1848 failed: 'Reaction did win, and thereby saved the reputation of the German revolution of 1848 (and of some others besides). It prevented the "revolution of the intellectuals" from consummating *la trahison des clercs.*' (pp.123–4) For most of us in the late 1940s, 1848 seemed to be a last — and lost — opportunity for the creation of a liberal Germany that might have avoided Bismarck's *Realpolitik,* Germany's 'bid for world power' in 1914 and Hitler's perversion of so many German values and his destructive racialism. Namier's *Revolution of the Intellectuals* forces us to question this assumption. And at a moment in history when there is widespread disillusion with revolutions in general and revolutions of the Left in particular and when in some circles 'liberal' has become a word of abuse, Namier's regret for an old order and his critique of the intellectuals of 1848 may well have a more favourable response than was to be expected when the lecture was written. And in any case even those who do not respond sympathetically to Namier's gloomy conservatism will find in the range and cogency of this book not only many shafts of light on the year 1848 itself but also a fresh insight into historical forces still at work in our own time.

London, May 1991

RALEIGH LECTURE ON HISTORY
Read 12 July 1944

1848:
THE REVOLUTION OF
THE INTELLECTUALS

by
L. B. NAMIER

I

ON 30 June 1847, in Rome, Father Joachim Ventura, in an oration delivered at the funeral of Daniel O'Connell, spoke of 'the revolution which threatens to encompass the globe'.[1] He voiced a widespread pre-cognition which was formative of the coming events. The revolution of 1848 was universally expected, and it was super-national as none before or after; it ran through, and enveloped, the core of Europe, 'the world' of the continental Europeans, which extended from the Channel ports to the frontiers of Russia, from Paris to Vienna. But it did not penetrate the two empires that flank the Continent—'What remains standing in Europe?' wrote Tsar Nicholas to Queen Victoria on 3 April 1848. 'Great Britain and Russia.'[2] 'What happened in London on April 10?' wondered the Polish poet, Count Krasiński. 'Thereby the fate of Europe will be decided for a long time to come.'[3] The 10th of April 1848 witnessed the eclipse of Chartism: in the most highly industrialized country the fight for the political and economic emancipation of the urban working classes passed into non-revolutionary channels. Russia, a perfect autocracy, with the largest peasant population living under a complete system of serfdom, presented the constitutional and social antithesis to England. In either country revolution would have had a homogeneous social character; in the middle zone it had not—and this is one of the outstanding features of 1848. Still, the European Continent responded to

[1] '. . . la rivoluzione, chi minaccia di fare il giro del globo. . . .' (see *Elogia funebre di Daniello O'Connell*, p. 62).

[2] *The Letters of Queen Victoria*, edited by A. C. Benson and Viscount Esher (1908), vol. ii, p. 196.

[3] *Listy Zygmunta Krasińskiego do Augusta Cieszkowskiego (Letters of Zygmunt Krasiński to August Cieszkowski)*, vol. ii, p. 19 (1912). The letter is dated Rome, 16 Apr. 1848, and in it, as printed, Krasiński asks about 'April 16th'; but the Chartist demonstration was on the 10th, and had Krasiński thought it to be on the 16th, he would have referred to it as happening 'to-day'.

the impulses and trends of the revolution with a remarkable uniformity, despite the differences of language and race, and in the political, social, and economic level of the countries concerned: but then the common denominator was ideological, and even literary, and there was a basic unity and cohesion in the intellectual world of the European Continent, such as usually asserts itself in the peak periods of its spiritual development. 1848 came not as an aftermath of war and defeat (as so many revolutions in the following century), but was the outcome of thirty-three creative years of European peace carefully preserved on a consciously counter-revolutionary basis. The revolution was born at least as much of hopes as of discontents. Odilon Barrot, under the July Monarchy one of the leaders of the Dynastic Opposition, writes: 'Never have nobler passions moved the civilized world, never has a more universal impulse of souls and hearts pervaded Europe from end to end: and yet all this was to result in failure. . . .'[1] And Lamartine, another of the makers and shipwrecks of 1848, describes it as 'the product of a moral idea, of reason, logic, sentiment, and of a desire . . . for a better order in government and society'.[2] The sequence and emphasis of his enumeration are significant. 1848 was primarily the revolution of the intellectuals—*la révolution des clercs*.

There was undoubtedly also an economic and social background to the revolution. Lean harvests in 1846 and 1847, and the potato disease, were causing intense misery in most parts of the Continent. Agrarian riots occurred in France where 1847 was long remembered as 'l'année du pain cher';[3] there was a 'potato revolution' in Berlin (complete with barricades), bread-riots in Stuttgart and Ulm, labour troubles in Vienna and in Bohemia, rank starvation in Silesia, &c. Count Galen,

---

[1] *Mémoires*, vol. ii (1876), p. 83. His shallowness, displayed in his *Mémoires*, does not render him less representative: he shared the naive enthusiasms of his time. Guizot writes about him (*Mémoires*, vol. ii (1859), p. 131): 'M. Odilon Barrot thought constitutional government easier, and men wiser, than they are; he banked too much on the virtue of free institutions to enlighten the nation, and on the lights of the nation to practise free institutions.' Falloux, in his *Mémoires d'un royaliste* (1888), says that Barrot died 'at the age of 80 [in 1873] without having taken stock of the Revolution of 1848 . . .'; and quotes a contemporary: 'C'est l'homme du monde qui pense le plus profondément . . . à rien!' And Proudhon: 'ce grand parleur, grand imbécile' (*Correspondence*, vol. ii (1875), p. 279; 25 Feb. 1848).

[2] *Histoire de la Révolution de 1848* (1849), vol. i, p. 3.

[3] See Albert Crémieux, *La Révolution de Février* (1912), p. 86.

the Prussian Minister, wrote from Kassel on 20 January 1847: 'The old year ended in scarcity, the new one opens with starvation. Misery, spiritual and physical, traverses Europe in ghastly shapes—the one without God, the other without bread. Woe if they join hands!'[1] Against this background economic or social conflicts were assuming a bitter, acute character. In most parts of the Austrian Empire, but more especially in Hungary and in Galicia, a final adjustment between big landowners and peasants was overdue: seignorial jurisdictions, *corvées*, and other remnants of serfdom had to be cleared away, and the title of the peasant to the land which he worked on his own, had to be established. Even in south-western Germany, on the confines of France and Switzerland, feudal survivals were fomenting agrarian revolt. All over Europe independent artisans were fighting their drawn-out losing battle against modern industry, especially desperate in the case of hand-spinners and weavers, or of carriers and bargees facing the competition of railways and steamboats: hence the attacks against modern machinery and means of transport at the outbreak of the revolution. On the other hand, the new class of factory workmen was starting its fight for a human existence. And when in 1847-8 a severe financial crisis set in, widespread unemployment ensued both among artisans and workmen, and among the large numbers of unskilled labour engaged on railway construction. Here was plenty of inflammable matter in ramshackle buildings. But was there a social-revolutionary movement at work, pursuing a feasible aim?

The French Revolution of 1789 and the Russian of 1917 were made and sustained by the converging action of the two greatest revolutionary forces: the people of the capital, effective through concentration at the very centre of government, and the peasant masses, invincible through their numbers, their dispersion, and the primitive, practical character of their demands (they never seek by revolt to establish new and higher forms of production, but to free themselves of burdens, or seize more land in order to cultivate it in their traditional, inadequate manner). In 1848 it was the proletariate of the quickly growing modern capitals[2] which brought the widespread discontents to a head: and 'accidents' and 'misunderstandings', epidemic in

---

[1] See Veit Valentin, *Geschichte der deutschen Revolution von 1848-49*, vol. i (1930), p. 192.

[2] The population of Paris increased from 774,000 in 1831 to 1,053,000 in 1846, reaching 1,226,980 if the suburbs are included; of Vienna from 248,000 in 1820 to 384,000 in 1840, 90 per cent. of the increase being non-indigenous

character—the 'fusillade' of the Boulevard des Capucins on 23 February, the salvo before the Vienna Landhaus on 13 March, and the 'two shots' fired in front of the Royal Palace in Berlin on the 18th—converted revolts into risings. For lack of support from other sections of the population, and of faith in themselves, the monarchical Governments collapsed under the impact of the working-class revolution. The conviction was universal that a change was long overdue. Aristocratic assemblies, such as the Hungarian Diet or the Bohemian Estates, were showing a progressive, oppositional spirit; in Italy, a liberal Pope, elected in 1846, set out to reform the administration of his States; in Prussia, the convocation of the United Diet in February 1847 (partially redeeming a promise of more than thirty years' standing) marked a step towards a constitutional régime. The abortive Polish revolution of 1846, the 'Sonderbund' War of 1847 in Switzerland, and, early in 1848, the outbreaks in Italy (or even the Lola Montez riots in Munich, an *opéra bouffe* suited to the place) were forerunners of a very much greater movement, symptoms of 'that mysterious force' which was to raise Europe. There was an intense consciousness of revolutionary tension, and no one seems to have had the strength, or even the will, to stand up to the storm when it broke. In exile Louis-Philippe declared that he had given way to forces of a moral order—*à une insurrection morale*; and on the eve of the revolution his queen and sons pressed for a change of system.[1]

(see M. Bach, *Geschichte der Wiener Revolution, 1848* (1898), p. 251). By 1848 Vienna and Berlin had populations of over 400,000. But there were only three provincial towns in France with a population of over 100,000 (Lyons, Marseilles, and Bordeaux); two in the Habsburg Monarchy (Budapest and Prague); and two in Germany (Hamburg and Breslau), besides four which were approaching the 100,000 mark (Munich, Dresden, Königsberg, and Cologne). The greatest number of city agglomerations (but of the premodern type) was to be found in Italy: Naples with a population of over 400,000, Rome, Palermo, Milan, and Turin with over 150,000, Venice, Genoa, Messina, Florence, and Bologna with about 100,000. (Even Great Britain had in 1851 only ten cities with over 100,000 inhabitants: London with 2,362,000; Liverpool, Glasgow, and Manchester with over 300,000; Birmingham with over 200,000; and Leeds, Edinburgh, Bristol, Sheffield, and Bradford with over 100,000.) In the capitals the garrisons were hardly adequate, if unaided, to keep down a serious rising. Their armament was not much superior to that which civilians, many of whom had received army training, could procure for themselves; and in street fighting these had a marked tactical superiority.

[1] About the Court opposition to Guizot, see his *Mémoires*, vol. viii, pp. 541–2 and 579–83; also Montalivet, *Fragments et Souvenirs*, vol. ii (1900), p. 115— he relates that some 8 or 10 days before the outbreak of the revolution, the

On 9 March 1848 King Wilhelm of Württemberg thus excused himself to Gorchakov, then Russian Minister in Stuttgart: 'Je ne puis pas monter à cheval contre les idées.'[1] In Vienna members of the Court and the Government were convinced of the need of Metternich's resignation before the cry for it was raised in the streets. Frederick William IV of Prussia more than surrendered to the revolution: he made a half-hearted attempt to place himself at its head. The monarchs gave in because they themselves were affected by the *Zeitgeist*—the ideas of a period 'whose active religion was politics';[2] and the middle classes, the foremost exponents of the new political creed, let them reel but did not overthrow them: with the sole exception of the Orleans dynasty, none lost its throne in 1848. The monarchs had merely to turn 'constitutional' and receive liberal intellectuals into political partnership. The mob had come out in revolt, moved by passions and distress rather than by ideas: they had no articulate aims, and no one will ever be able to supply a rational explanation of what it was they fought for, or what made them fight. Proudhon writes: 'Le 24 février a été fait sans idée.'[3] The working classes touched off, and the middle classes cashed in on it. There was something incongruous about the opening scene of the revolution of 1848.

II

In France and Germany the middle classes comprised probably half the nation,[4] and were ever ready to comport themselves as if they formed the whole. Self-assertive but timid, and individualistic in outlook, they were not given to mass-action, and watched popular movements with misgivings. When in Vienna and Berlin they demanded 'arms for the people' (*Volksbewaffnung*), they meant for men of property or education,

Queen, influenced by the Princes (Joinville, Aumâle, and Montpensier) sent for him, and begged him to make a supreme effort to persuade the King to get rid of Guizot; Montalivet replied that she alone had a chance of succeeding. See further Crémieux, *La Révolution de Février*, about the line adopted by the Queen and the Princes in the afternoon of 23 Feb.

[1] Valentin, op. cit., vol. i, p. 352.
[2] 'La religion active de nos jours, c'est la politique', Circourt, *Souvenirs d'une mission à Berlin en 1848* (1908), vol. i, p. 310.
[3] *Correspondence*, vol. ii, p. 280.
[4] In France the *bourgeois* starts lower in the social scale, and extends higher, than in most countries; and in 1848 he was sharply separated from the upper classes and the people. For the middle classes in Germany, see Valentin, op. cit., vol. i, pp. 289–96; his estimate for Prussia includes in them two-thirds of the population.

fit guardians of the existing social order as much as of the newly acquired freedoms: in both cities workmen, day labourers, or journeymen were excluded from the National Guard.[1] The terms 'Communists' and 'proletariate' (since embalmed in the Marxian nomenclature) were in general use, and evoked intense, exaggerated, fears.[2] The very absence of a definite programme, perhaps not unjustifiably, tended to increase them: for it pointed to a class-war of blind hatreds. On 13 March cases of murder and looting occurred in the Vienna suburbs, though the mob which attacked factories and destroyed their machinery carefully refrained from pilfering. Even when during the siege of Vienna, in October 1848, the nationalist radicals fought side by side with men from the working-class suburbs, distrust persisted. Smolka, a Pole who at that time presided over the Austrian Parliament, in a letter to his wife on the 30th, mentions fears of looting by the 'proletariate' as they were being forced back on to the Inner City. 'I was sure that this would not happen,' he writes; 'I have come to know the integrity and honour of the poor people of this town: their exemplary behaviour deserves the highest praise.'[3] All over Europe the middle classes paid lip-service to the 'people' and its cause, but never felt altogether secure or happy in its company. They would emulate the humanitarian endeavours of the Convention of 1792 (described by one of its members as 'an assembly of philosophers engaged on preparing the happiness

---

[1] When on 14 March, leading Vienna citizens called at the Burg to demand the formation of a National Guard—which they obtained after some resistance—both sides were agreed from the outset to exclude 'proletarians'. When the same day, workmen gathered before the Arsenal demanded arms, the university students were in favour of giving them, but the citizens violently protested against it, 'as they feared that the bloody riots of the Mariahilf district would be repeated in the Inner City and its immediate suburbs' (see Reschauer, *Das Jahr 1848. Geschichte der Wiener Revolution* (1872), pp. 383–4; also M. Bach, op. cit.). The exclusion of the workmen was embodied in the Statute of the Vienna National Guard of 10 Apr., which the Committee of Fifty (*der Fünfziger-Ausschuss*) of the Pre-Parliament (*Vorparlament*) recommended to other towns as a model (see Valentin, op. cit., vol. i, p. 522).

[2] Anton Springer, a contemporary, writing in 1863, speaks about 'the exaggerated fear evoked [in 1846–8] by the social movement' (*einer — damals über Gebühr gefürchteten — sozialen Bewegung*); see his *Geschichte Oesterreichs seit dem Wiener Frieden, 1809* (vol. i, p. 532), to this day perhaps the best comprehensive work on the Austrian revolution of 1848.

[3] See S. Smolka, *Dziennik F. Smolki, 1848–49, w listach do żony* (*The Diary of F. Smolka 1848–49, in Letters to his Wife*) (1913), p. 113.

of the world') but they were determined to avoid the sequel. They had faith in democracy, parliamentary democracy, and trusted that the people whom they had enfranchised would return them in elections; and then it should stand behind them, and await the outcome of their deliberations. They wanted the revolution to enter like the ghost in Dickens's *Christmas Carol*, with a flaming halo round its head and a big extinguisher under its arm.

Baron von Meyendorff, Russian Ambassador in Berlin, wrote on 25 March to Field-Marshal Prince Paskevich, Governor-General of Russian Poland, that the first stage of the social revolution in Prussia had closed with 'the triumph of the *bourgeois* allied to the workman over the Government'; but now the *bourgeois* will wish for order and security, while the workman will attack property: if fighting breaks out between the National Guard and the workmen in Paris, and the workmen win, the conflict will spread to Berlin.[1] It was still an open question whether the revolution of 1848 would assume a social character, or be confined within political channels: and it was primarily in France that this had to be decided. There, on the political side, 1848 was deeply tinged with historical and literary reminiscences, and followed a revolutionary routine. 'On cherchait . . . à se réchauffer aux passions de nos pères, sans pouvoir y parvenir', writes Alexis de Tocqueville; 'on imitait leurs gestes et leurs poses tels qu'on les avait vus sur le théâtre, ne pouvant imiter leur enthousiasme ou ressentir leur fureur.'[2] On the social side the need of improving the lot of 'the labouring poor' was acknowledged. Most of the candidates at the French general election of April 1848 placed 'l'organisation du travail' foremost among their promises, and proclaimed it their principal concern, but failed to define it: it stood 'surcharged with epithets and obscured by metaphors',[3] admitted as a problem and descanted about in a manner which suggests ignorance, embarrassment, and apprehension. Meantime, the stage was

---

[1] Peter von Meyendorff, *Politischer und privater Briefwechsel 1826–63*, edited by Otto Hoetzsch (1923), vol. ii, pp. 53–4.

[2] *Souvenirs* (1893), p. 75. The secondary, imitative character of the February Revolution finds direct, or unconscious, illustration in practically all contemporary memoirs—and their name is legion—but nowhere is it so brilliantly analysed as in Tocqueville.

[3] See Henri Moysset, 'L'Organisation du Travail dans les Professions de Foi' in *La Révolution de 1848. Bulletin de la Société d'Histoire de la Révolution de 1848*, vol. iii. Most candidates, though not all, issued these programmatic declarations, and Moysset has analysed some 4,000 of them.

being set for Civil War. The demonstration by the 'bonnets à poil' (the National Guards from the Paris middle-class district) on 16 March, and the counter-demonstration of the workmen the next day, the collision on 16 April, the abortive *coup* of the extremists on 15 May against the National Assembly, were preludes to the June Days—'that insurrection . . .', writes Tocqueville, 'the greatest and most singular . . . in our history', in which 100,000 insurgents fought 'without a war-cry, without chiefs, or a standard, and yet with a cohesion and a military skill which surprised the oldest officers'. 'This formidable revolt was not the work of a group of conspirators, but the rising of one part of the population against the other. Women took part in it as much as men . . . they hoped for victory to ease the lot of their husbands, and help to bring up their children.' 'This was . . . not a political struggle . . . but class-war, a kind of slave-war. It forms the most characteristic feature of the February Revolution.' Without it the French revolution of 1848 becomes senseless: there remains the gaping void of its politics.

No wonder if after June people started asking themselves what the February Days had been about, and asserted that the revolution, which had been predicted months, if not years, ahead,[1] was an accident, a meaningless, yet fatal, accident. 'A revolution without cause or properly defined aim', writes Odilon Barrot;[2] '. . . which no one wanted the day before, and to which everyone seemed to resign himself on the day after.'[3] 'A revolution out of proportion to its cause', runs Falloux's correcting version;[4] 'it interrupted a development which was slow, but did advance.' 'A miserable and childish affair, a banquet which should have been allowed provided it did not interfere with the street traffic, sufficed to destroy so much noble work and open an abyss which we have not yet fathomed', wrote Ernest Renan in 1859.[5] The year 1848 in France carried the two basic political ideas of the Great Revolution to their logical conclusion: equality was achieved in universal suffrage, and the sovereignty of the people in the Republic. The development which it interrupted, and the noble work which it

---

[1] See H. Monin, 'Le Pressentiment Social, à propos de la Révolution de 1848 en France', in the *Revue Internationale de Sociologie*, vol. v (1897).

[2] *Mémoires*, vol. ii, p. 66.   [3] Ibid., p. 70.

[4] *Mémoires d'un royaliste*, vol. i, p. 217.

[5] In the essay 'Philosophie de l'histoire contemporaine', reprinted in *Questions contemporaines* (1863), p. 55.

destroyed, were what in other continental countries the revolution, on its political side,[1] aspired to attain: parliamentary
government and political liberty under a constitutional monarchy. But the intellectuals, red or pink, had yet to learn that
the parliamentary system is based on an articulation of society,
and not on levelling it down, and that, with social superiorities
discredited and the political structure broken, the field is open,
or rather the void is prepared, for plebiscitarian dictatorships.
Montalembert said in Parliament, on 19 October 1849: 'The
kings have reascended their thrones, liberty has not reascended
hers—the throne which she had in our hearts.'[2]

III

The June Days heightened the fears, the self-consciousness,
and the determination of the middle-classes throughout Europe.
The National Guard in Vienna came out against the workmen
in August and September, and when on 18 September the
Frankfort Parliament called in Austrian and Prussian troops to
put down a popular riot in the town, the Provisional Government of the new Germany (yet unborn) naively 'believed . . .
through their victory to have justified their existence'.[3] But, in
fact, none of the popular revolts in central and east-central
Europe had a clear class character: there was a growing element

---

[1] The Memorandum of the Czech Members of the Austrian Parliament
about the policy which they had pursued in 1848–9, apparently drawn up
by the historian and politician, F. Palacký, distinguishes between the social,
political, and national elements in the revolution, making 'political' cover
the problem of self-government and the freedoms (see Palacký, *Gedenkblätter*,
pp. 190–1). This seems a useful classification.

[2] I cannot enter here into the reasons why parliamentary government
failed in France and the July Monarchy collapsed. The most succinct
explanation of its fall was given by Sainte-Beuve: 'Les d'Orléans n'étaient
ni un principe ni une gloire nationale, ils étaient une utilité, un expédient . . .'
(*Nouveaux Lundis*, vol. i, 14 Oct. 1861, essay on Guizot's *Mémoires*). The
'juste milieu' was not even a workable compromise, for the Legitimists,
looking upon it as a 'profanation of monarchy', split the Conservative
forces; they openly rejoiced at the downfall of Louis-Philippe. Parliament,
like monarchy, must command respect in order to exist and work. The
stories about 'parliamentary corruption' under Guizot are more significant
than convincing; such stories crop up regularly when a parliamentary
régime totters to its fall (and is about to be succeeded by one even more
distinguished for political mendacity and mendicity).

[3] Valentin, op. cit., vol. ii, pp. 168–9. For the pride which, for instance,
Anton von Schmerling, the quasi-Premier, took in the putting down of the
riots, see his letters of 22 and 24 Sept., printed in Arneth, *Anton Ritter von
Schmerling* (1895), pp. 213–14.

of national radicalism in them. Nor can the three earlier counter-revolutionary *coups*—the bombardment of Cracow on 26 April, the fighting in Posnania in April and May, and the bombardment of Prague by Windischgrätz on 17 June—be classed with the June Days, even though they worked in a parallel direction: their background was national.

⟶   The only other outbreak of a class character, negating the national principle, was the Galician *jacquerie* of 1846,[1] which deeply influenced the development of the revolution of 1848 in the Habsburg Monarchy, and caused governments, parliaments, and the landed classes themselves, to hasten the reforms completing the emancipation of the peasants from feudal burdens and jurisdictions: the issue was decided before it was joined.

Among the Poles and the Magyars, the gentry—an exceedingly numerous body[2] which has hardly its equivalent in any

[1] It is often stated that Ruthene peasants massacred Polish big landowners: in reality the outbreak was almost entirely limited to districts of western Galicia whose peasantry speaks Polish.

[2] A. de Fenyes, in his *Statistik des Koenigreichs Ungarn* (1843) puts the number of 'gentry' in Hungary at 550,000, in a total population of less than 13 millions. This estimate is borne out by the fact that in the *comitats* (shires), in which the suffrage was limited to the gentry, there were at that time 136,000 voters. Thus there was one *nobilis* to some 23 *roturiers* in the total population, and 1 to 9 among the Magyars.

For Poland there are no reliable statistics of the gentry. In the book on *Poland* (1945), edited by Bernadotte Schmitt and R. J. Kerner, Halecki puts the gentry at nearly 'one-tenth of all the inhabitants' (p. 44), Zawacki at 'nearly 12 per cent. of the total population' (p. 334), while Radwan puts the petty gentry alone at 'around 15 per cent. of the total population' (p. 219). None names the date, and hence the exact territory, to which his estimate refers, and all three estimates seem therefore equally vague and unreliable; and Radwan's is certainly too high. On the other hand, specific nineteenth-century estimates for Galicia are frequently too low: the political privileges of the gentry having disappeared, the petty gentry tend to be left out of account. Thus Fenyes states that in Galicia there was, in 1840, 1 member of the gentry to 68 'non-gentry' (for Lombardy he puts the proportion at 1 to 300, for German Austria as 1 to 350, and for Bohemia as 1 to 828). Ostaszewski-Barański, *Rok Złudzeń, 1848* (*The Year of Mirages, 1848*), p. 75, puts the number of the Galician gentry in 1848 at 30,454, in a total population of 4,920,300; Wiesiołowski in his *Pamiętnik z r. 1845–6* (1868) (*Diary of 1845–6*), p. 7, puts it even lower: at only 12,000 in 1833.

So much, however, is certain: that among the Poles and the Magyars practically the entire educated class, the only one with a marked national consciousness, was of gentry extraction, but that among the gentry there were large numbers of men who, except for their national and class consciousness, differed but little from the peasants.

other nation—replaced the middle classes. It was much more effective than these as a national revolutionary force: bred to arms for generations, the gentry had the spirit and traditions of fighting men. Having, together with the magnates, enjoyed a monopoly of power in the State, they became the sole exponents of the national idea. Moreover, as the Polish gentry-nation had absorbed the landed classes of Lithuania, White Russia, and of most of the Ukraine, covering territory about three times that inhabited by a Polish peasantry, the greatness of Poland was bound up with the caste rule of the gentry; with certain variants the same was true of Hungary. But such was the distance that separated the Polish gentry even from the Polish-speaking peasants, that these did not, on the whole, consider themselves part of the nation of their masters.[1] Ziemiałkowski, one of the chief leaders of the Austrian Poles in 1848 and for nearly half a century after, wrote as late as March 1865: '. . . in Galicia the peasants do not think of Poland and do not want Poland, while the town population only begins to awaken from its lethargy.'[2] And things were, if anything, worse while heavy *corvées* and patrimonial jurisdictions still poisoned relations between the big landowners and their peasants, and were being deliberately exploited by a hostile Austrian bureaucracy.[3]

In 1845 the Polish Democrats were preparing, largely under the direction of *émigré* organizations in western Europe, a national rising against all the three Partitioning Powers. It was, of need, worked in a conspiratorial manner which helped to hide, even from the leaders, the utter insufficiency of their

---

[1] Like most generalizations, this, too, has its exceptions. Even in Galicia, in 1846, there were in a few places the beginnings of a national movement among the peasants, usually owing to the influence of the clergy. Under Prussia and Russia the religious contrast, by identifying Polish nationality with Roman Catholicism, favoured the growth of a Polish national consciousness, though even there the class antagonism exercised for a long time a retarding influence.

[2] *Pamiętniki (Memoirs)* (1904), part 4, p. 187; see also L. von Mises, *Die Entwicklung des gutsherrlich-bäuerlichen Verhältnisses in Galizien, 1772–1848* (1902), pp. 104–5.

[3] Thus, for instance, Czetsch-Lindenwald, the Austrian *Kreishauptmann* (District Commissioner) of Przemyśl, wrote in a report dated 18 Apr. 1846: 'To remove the chief source of hatred between the peasants and the gentry, namely the patrimonial jurisdictions, would undermine the foundations of government'; quoted by Mises (op. cit., p. 94, n. 1) who, however, tries to defend the Austrian Government against the accusation of having deliberately continued the system of patrimonial jurisdictions in order to poison relations between the landowners and the peasants.

resources and the visionary futility of their schemes. In 1830–1 the Polish leaders, aristocrats or gentry, could not bring themselves to appeal to the peasants by proclaiming their complete emancipation. The men of 1845–6, though themselves of the gentry class,[1] saw the mistake: comparing the weakness and failure of the Polish effort with the victorious *élan* of the French revolutionary armies (when these, too, faced seemingly hopeless odds), they concluded that only by raising social-revolutionary forces could they vanquish the organized might of their enemies and oppressors.[2] Besides, they dreamt of a world revolution and war, and figured a system of world politics pivoting on Poland, gyrating round her, consummated in her resurrection, and culminating in her renewed greatness.[3] Such fancies and conceits inspired Polish activities—then, and ever since. And the extraordinary pattern emerged of a nation, essentially aristocratic and martial, steeped in the gentry legend of the sword, with its greatness founded on latifundia and their owners, and yet plunging, from patriotic motives, into social-revolutionary action.[4] The Poles have, by turns, been exalted as paladins of liberty and decried as reactionaries. They are neither: but a case *sui generis*, as is every nation, though more complex owing to the complexities of their position.[5]

[1] Mierosławski writes about the Polish *émigrés* (of whom he was one): 'They all were gentry, defeated gentry doing penance, redeemed by wounds of the soul and body—but gentry'; see *Powstanie poznańskie w roku 1848* (*The Posnanian Revolution of 1848*), 2nd ed. (1860), p. 39.

[2] The Prussian forces stationed in Posnania in 1846 were put at only 4,160, the Austrian in Galicia at about 30,000; but of these a mere 6,000 were stationed in western Galicia. A powerful popular movement might indeed have overwhelmed them in the initial stages.

[3] Ladislas Mickiewicz, son of the poet, wrote in 1870, in his introduction to *La politique du dix-neuvième siècle* (a collection of political essays by his father): '. . . il n'est pas plus possible de faire de la bonne politique sans la Pologne que de rêver une pure morale sans Dieu' (p. lxxv).

[4] Piłsudski was the last, and the most successful, of these revolutionary knights-errant; his 'socialism' was a modern variant on the creed of the Polish 'democrats' of 1848 and 1863. But as early as 1907 he tried to establish a para-military dictatorship within the Polish Socialist Party; and after 1918, and still more after 1926, he entered Napoleon's path without Napoleon's power or justification. It would be unfair to describe him, or even his epigoni, as Fascists—the meanness of Fascism attached much rather to his opponents of the Dmowski school. Piłsudski's was a nobler tradition; but for that very reason dangerous—to this day Polish Socialism is tinged with militarist Imperialism, disguised by political fantasies—an anachronistic Polish quasi-Bonapartism.

[5] In Feb. 1849 one of the Czech leaders, Rieger, said in the Austrian

The leaders of the Polish conspiracy met in Cracow in January 1846. Mierosławski[1] was designated military commander, and the outbreak was fixed for the night of 21–2 February. In Russian Poland, suffering from the aftermath of 1830–1 and the consequent oppression, the movement never got going; in Posnania it was nipped in the bud by the arrest of the leaders, including Mierosławski, on 12 and 14 February; in Austrian Poland some, seeing that the rising had failed elsewhere, wished to countermand it, others to hasten it. It broke out in a few places during the night of 18–19 February. But the authorities in Galicia, scared of revolution and filled with hatred of the Poles, most effectively parried the blow: in a tense atmosphere, full of fear and rumours,[2] they called on the peasants to rise

Constitutional Committee: 'The Polish gentry are only seemingly liberal, in their hearts they are reactionary' (see *Protokolle des Verfassungs-Ausschusses im Oesterreichischen Reichstag, 1848–9*, edited by A. Springer, 1885, p. 186). This was a protest of a Czech democrat sitting on the Right, against the 'liberal' claims of Polish gentry-representatives on the Left: but it over-simplified the problem.

[1] Mierosławski was born in 1814, of a French mother—through her *un Gascognard*. He was educated at a military school, and as a youth fought in the Polish Revolution of 1830–1. He had command of the revolutionary forces in Posnania in Mar.–May 1848, in Sicily towards the end of the year, and in Baden in 1849; he was Commander-in-Chief during the first month of the Polish Revolution of 1863—a series of ephemeral, or even futile, ventures. His merits as a soldier are open to doubt. Circourt, in a letter of 28 Mar. 1848, credits him with 'merely the qualities of a stage hero'; and although Circourt's opinions about Poles must be treated with caution, it seems that Mierosławski hardly deserved the prominence which he enjoyed as a military leader of revolutions. He was a prolific writer of 'baroque exuberance', and his literary output seems to have unduly enhanced his military reputation. S. Kieniewicz thus sums up his career in a sound and well-balanced character sketch: 'He was a general who never commanded; he believed in the people and had absolutely no knowledge of them; he loved his country and did it the greatest amount of harm.' See *Społeczeństwo polskie w powstaniu poznańskiem 1848 roku* (*Polish Society in the Posnania Rising of 1848*) (1935), pp. 67–71.

[2] In 1845–6 some of those curious pre-revolutionary tremors, resembling *la grande peur* of 1789, were noted in Galicia. See, for instance, Wiesiołowski, op. cit., pp. 33–4, on the rumours current early in 1845, especially in the districts of Wadowice and Bochnia, that on Good Friday there would be a massacre of the gentry by the peasants, who, in turn, stood in fear of an undefined 'great danger'. Many of the gentry fled into the towns, and some even appealed to the Austrian officials for protection; 'on the other hand, peasants armed with scythes and flails mounted guard at night, and would stop strangers on the roads, believing themselves threatened by "treason".' It was also widely believed by the peasants that their final emancipation was impending, and that, indeed, a decree freeing them had been signed by the Emperor but filched by the gentry.

B

against their masters.   There was the pretence of a patriotic
Austrian movement against the insurgents ('Communists', or
'Jacobins' as Metternich called them): in reality it was an
indiscriminate *jacquerie*, which claimed some 2,000 victims.
J. Breinl von Wallerstern, District Commissioner of Tarnów,
paid money to the peasants for 'insurgents' brought in, dead or
alive.[1] An order is preserved, issued by the District Commissioner
of Lvov, Milbacher, which incites to murder.[2] On 23 February,
five days after the *jacquerie* had started, Baron Krieg, head of the
Galician Administration, ordered district commissioners 'to
send officials to the villages and call on the peasant-serfs to
co-operate in resisting and apprehending rebels'.[3] Colonel
Benedek (of Königgrätz fame, 1866), when taking the field
against the insurgents, was accompanied by crowds of peasants,
who had been promised 220 lb. of salt each,[4] and a bonus of
5 gulden (8s. 4d.) for every insurgent captured (the battle of
Gdów, miserably mismanaged by the Poles, degenerated into
a sheer massacre of them by the peasants).

The Galician events produced horror and stupefaction
among the upper classes of western Austria. A German big
landowner, settled in West Galicia, stated in a memorandum
of 16 April 1846, which he wrote at the request of the

[1] It was alleged at the time that bonuses were paid on a *per capita* basis.
So far I have found no conclusive evidence to prove it. But what is admitted
—that the peasants who brought in so-called insurgents, dead, wounded,
or captured, were paid for 'loss of time', maintenance, 'transport', &c.—is
bad enough, even if less blatant.

[2] Care seems to have been taken to destroy compromising documents,
but this one survived through a curious chance. It is published in facsimile
by B. Łoziński, *Szkice z historji Galicyi w XIX wieku* (*Essays in Galician History
in the 19th Century*) (1913), pp. 334–5, and runs as follows:

Reg. No. 74. To the Mandatory Błocki,
    You are directed to summon all peasants with their scythes, order them
to apprehend the rebels, and should these offer resistance, to do them in.
Soldiers on leave should help. Commissary Klosson will come and give
assistance to the stout peasants of Horożana.
    With a hundred peasants you should be able to wipe out a hundred
such rascals (*Spitzbuben*); in the district of Tarnów the peasants have
achieved it; they caught 108, including four Counts, and killed 27. You
have an opportunity to prove your attachment to His Majesty, and I
expect it from you. Courage and energy will bring condign punishment
on the rebels. Report everything to me.
    Lvov, February 22, 1846.   MILBACHER.

[3] Łoziński, op. cit., p. 337.

[4] From the neighbouring salt-mines of Wieliczka, owned by the Government.

highest government circles in Vienna: 'I see in the present condition of Galicia, the first victory of Communism; others must
follow. . . . The peasants, who in their looting and brigandage
have met with no resistance, have come to realize, or even to
over-rate, their collective strength.'[1] Gradually officials responsible for the events were withdrawn, and in 1847, Count Franz
Stadion, one of the most enlightened and efficient Austrian
administrators, was appointed Governor of Galicia.[2] But the
Austrian Government could not punish the peasants for the
outrages—judicial proceedings against gentry insurgents were
quick and sharp, against peasant murderers and looters dilatory
and most lenient; in the end the political amnesty of 1848 was
made to draw a veil also over the Galician *jacquerie*. Still less
could the Government reduce its late allies to their previous
state of subjection to the big landowners, and during the two
years preceding March 1848 fumbling attempts were made at
resettling relations between landowners and peasants. The
agrarian problem had been opened up, and not for Galicia
alone.

Frederick William IV, in talking to a Polish delegation from
Posnania on 23 March 1848 told them that 'one of the highest
placed personages in Austria' had said to him: 'The disturbances
in Italy and the troubles in Switzerland have done us a great
deal of harm, and the financial crisis has caused us many
difficulties, but nothing has been so disastrous for our Monarchy
as the Polish peasants rising against the gentry in defence of the
Government.'[3]

IV

From the outset of the revolution of 1848 there was absolute
unanimity throughout the Habsburg dominions that a thorough-
going emancipation of the peasants was of paramount urgency:
the work half-accomplished by Joseph II during the decade
preceding the French Revolution, and shelved by his successors,
had to be completed. There was a scramble for priority

---

[1] Łoziński, op. cit., p. 271.

[2] Ibid., p. 463. A rough draft of his report of 28 Dec. 1847, highly critical
of the Galician bureaucracy, contains a sentence deleted from its final text:
it admits that some officials 'had incited the peasants to excesses, or even
participated in them'.

[3] See *Im Polen-Aufruhr, 1846–8. Aus den Papieren eines Landrats* (1898).
The author is identified by W. Kohte, *Deutsche Bewegung und preussische
Politik im Posener Lande* (1931), p. 26, as Juncker von Ober-Conreuth,
Landrat of Czarnikau.

between National Committees, Assemblies, and the Government
in initiating it, each desiring to placate and gratify the peasant
masses, and to attach them to its cause. The demand for the
abolition of the 'robot',[1] figures prominently in the programme
drafted by the Prague National Committee on 11–12 March;
and even the aristocratic Bohemian Estates favoured a speedy
convocation of a Diet which would deal with the problem.
When the news of the Vienna Revolution reached Budapest,
a national programme in twelve points was drawn up by
the Radical Opposition, of which the seventh demanded the
abolition of feudal rights and burdens; and on 18 March this
was voted by the Hungarian Parliament, although it was composed almost exclusively of representatives of the aristocracy
and the landed gentry—they merely placed the claim of landowners to compensation 'under the protecting shield of the
national honour', while the clergy voluntarily renounced its
tithes. Similarly, the Address to the Emperor drafted at Lvov
on 18 March, and signed by large numbers of Polish big landowners, declared for removing all survivals of serfdom.

Fear and foresight quickened resolutions which were enjoined by common sense. The Hungarian Parliament acted
under the pressing threat of a peasant rising, while Kossuth
wished to gain over the peasant masses, and also reckoned with
the effect which such measures might have on Croatia. When
at the end of March some Conservative leaders of the Magyar
magnates prepared a memorandum for the Archduke Palatine,
analysing possible ways of dealing with the Hungarian Revolution, they warned Vienna against admitting a repetition of the
Galician events of 1846, be it by a mere withdrawal of regular
troops from Hungary: for the loyal Conservative elements in
Hungary would be the foremost sufferers. And when in April
the Hungarian Government demanded the return of Hungarian regiments from Moravia and Galicia (which they
needed primarily against the Serbs and Croats), among the
reasons which they chose to name they quoted cases of agrarian

---

[1] *Robota* means in Slav languages 'labour', and serfdom in Austria having
been most burdensome in the Slav provinces, the word 'robot' came to
denote in the Austro-German vocabulary labour dues of serf origin: it is
hardly correct to speak of 'serfdom' anywhere in Austria after the reforms
of Joseph II had emancipated the persons of the peasants, and a different
description is required for the agrarian problem as it existed in 1848. The
word 'robot' having entered the English language through Čapek's famous
play, it might perhaps be possible to admit the expression 'robot problem'
into the English historical vocabulary.

disturbances in certain Magyar districts, and the danger of their spreading.

Naturally even more outspoken were the Poles in this matter. In the Lvov Address of 18 March they declared that nowhere was 'a powerful development of national forces' more necessary than in Galicia, seeing that 'the deplorable events of 1846 have produced so great a rift between landowners and peasants as to threaten a complete dissolution of all social ties'. The sixth of the thirteen points of the Lvov Address demanded 'a general and most speedy arming of the towns to safeguard peace, order, and the security of persons and property'. And the amended address[1] of 6 April, while demanding a Polish 'national army', asked that in the meantime the Austrian troops stationed in Galicia should be used to maintain peace and security in the villages. When on 21 March a rumour spread in Lvov that the peasants were coming, the cry arose: 'Give us arms, for they are out to massacre us!' The National Guard in Galicia was to be formed only in places with over 1,000 inhabitants (and even there workmen and journeymen were excluded): no one would have wished or dared to arm the peasants.[2] Everywhere in Austria serf labour and dues ceased to be rendered after the outbreak of the revolution. In Galicia the Polish National Council on 17 April issued an appeal to the big landowners for a voluntary renunciation (which was done by a certain number). But while the agrarian settlement in most provinces of Austria was left to the forthcoming Constituent Assembly, in Galicia a decree was published on 22 April by the Governor, Count Franz Stadion, announcing that as from 15 May all serf labour and dues were to cease 'against compensation to be

---

[1] See below, p. 30.

[2] The Governor of Galicia, Count Franz Stadion, though decried as an enemy of the Poles, warned Vienna against invoking or accepting the active support of the peasants. B. Łoziński, in his book on Count Agenor Gołuchowski, *Agenor hrabia Gołuchowski, w pierwszym okresie rządów swoich, 1846–1859* (1901), tries to do justice to Stadion, who wrote on 12 Apr. 1848 (p. 71): 'As yet the peasant is quiet, but watches every step of the hated gentry; he shows devotion to the Government, but his help must never be reckoned with: for if it were invited, there could be no thought of controlling that savage force. Hatred will be the motive, and will turn the peasants against the big land-owners and gentry. They will not try to support or restore peace and order, but will take to murder and looting.' And again on 27 Apr.: 'The peasants are devoted to the Government but should not be roused, for I cannot say it too often, or too emphatically, that defence of the Government would be a mere pretext for murder, looting, and incendiarism.'

fixed at a future date at the expense of the State'.[1] 'By this praiseworthy act', writes Friedjung, 'he retained the loyalty of the Galician peasantry for Emperor and State, and nipped in the bud any attempt to separate from Austria.'[2]

The reactionary circles [writes Anton Springer] had no reason to fear the middle classes, which in all the big towns, and especially in Vienna, had shown themselves politically immature and lacking in independence and energy. . . . With the peasants alone they had to count as with a power. . . .

The absolutist *régime* had failed to meet the wishes and to attend to the interests of the peasants, who therefore turned against it. From the revolution they expected a favourable settlement; they understood neither programmes nor manifestos, and felt no zeal for constitutional rights or democratic principles; but they knew that they could name the price for their support, and that on all sides there was the desire to fulfil their demands. The revolution remained strong only so long as the peasants expected it to improve their condition and to secure their freedom; reaction could not set in until the emancipation of the peasants had been accomplished, and the peasants had lost interest in politics. . . . The peasants were the power behind the revolution, and the problem of 'robot' its pivot.[3]

In the Austrian Parliament of 1848 there were 92 peasants in a total of 383 members—and there would have been many more but for the Czechs and Ruthenes, both at that time essentially peasant nations: the Czech intelligentsia and the Ruthene Uniat priests were so close to the peasant class in origin and interests that many were returned in lieu of peasants. Thus while Upper Austria counted 13 peasants among its 16 deputies, and Galicia (almost half of it Polish) and the Bukovina had 38 among 108, Bohemia and Moravia had only 16 peasants among 138 members. In the Prussian Diet a total of 402 members included 68 peasants, but about half of them were from Silesia, a province with a large Polish population—the only one in Prussia which in 1848 experienced a peasant rising. The Frankfort Parliament had only one single peasant among its members, and he was a Pole from Upper Silesia: agrarian problems in the constituent States were outside the jurisdiction

[1] The original German text reads: 'gegen eine künftig zu ermittelnde Entschädigung auf Kosten des Staates.' According to Ostaszewski-Barański, op. cit., pp. 178–9, this was mistranslated into Polish as 'at the expense of the Government', so as to impress once more on the peasant that it was from the Government that he derived all the blessings.

[2] *Oesterreich von 1848 bis 1860*, 4th ed. (1918), vol. i, p. 347.

[3] *Geschichte Oesterreichs seit dem Wiener Frieden 1809* (1865), vol. ii, p. 366.

of the German National Assembly, and German unity was of no interest to the peasants.

In the third session of the Vienna Parliament, on 26 July 1848, a resolution demanding the immediate abolition of all rights and duties derived from the subjection of the peasants (*das Unterthänigkeits-Verhältniss*) was unanimously carried. Controversy was limited to the question of compensation, the peasants passionately opposing any payments to their masters. Of the laughter which 'frequently interrupted the oratorical attempts of peasants', writes Springer,[1] there was none when 'in the deeply disturbed assembly a Galician peasant, Kapusciak, gave his views on the robot problem—in a clumsy manner, in broken German, but with clenched fists and rolling eyes, and with a wild hatred against the gentry'.

Yes, the nobleman has treated the peasant lovingly [said Kapusciak]. After having been made to work all week, he was entertained on the Sunday—chained and locked up in the cowshed, so that he should work still harder the next week. Yes, the nobleman is humane, for he encourages the tired robot-peasant with the whip, and if the peasant complains that his draft-animals are too weak to perform the prescribed labour, he is told: 'Then harness yourself and your wife'. . . . Three hundred steps from the manor-house, he has humbly to take off his hat . . . and if the poor peasant wants to mount the stairs, he is told to stay in the court-yard, for he stinks. . . . And for such ill-treatment are we now to pay compensation? I say: No!! The whips which came down on our heads and tired bodies must suffice. Let these be the compensation of the masters.

When on 7 September the Emancipation Act passed its last reading, the peasant masses lost further interest in Parliament;[2] and it did not revive even when reaction swept away most of the work of the revolution, for the agrarian settlement was left

---

[1] Op. cit., vol. ii, pp. 420–1.

[2] Ibid., p. 249. In the First Russian Duma the question was once discussed in a party meeting of the Constitutional Democrats (the so-called 'Cadets'), which should be given priority, the constitutional or the agrarian problem? Shmarya Levin, member for Vilna, though ignorant of the Austrian precedent, told his Russian colleagues the following story: 'On the Sabbath, pious Jews must not strike a light, nor even ask a non-Jew to do it, though they may have it done for them. The better-off will let the light burn all night. But during a long winter night, such a Jew found that it had gone out. He wanted to read. So he woke up his peasant servant, and asked: "Ivan, would you like a drink?" "Sure, I would." "But it's so dark, I can't find the bottle." So Ivan lit the candle—exactly what the Jew wanted. But after Ivan had had his glass of vodka, in his innocence he put out the light. Be careful or Ivan will blow out your candle.'

untouched. The Minister of the Interior, Alexander Bach (who in less than a year changed from a Radical into a champion of autocracy), was of peasant origin, and knew that there was no going back on the promises and concessions made to the peasants.[1] Even Prince Alfred Windischgrätz, the political general who at one time had set up military control over the civilian Government, failed to obtain modifications in favour of the big landowners. 'The most pronounced Communist', he told the Emperor in February 1850, 'has not yet dared to demand what Your Majesty's Government now enact.'[2]

There were no peasants on the Constitutional Committee set up by the Parliament of 1848, and it discussed their political rôle with naive freedom.[3] 'The town is the cradle of democracy'. argued K. Mayer, a Moravian German; 'democratic convictions are to be found only in towns', declared the Pole Ziemiałkowski; 'once the agrarian problem is settled, the peasant turns conservative, or even reactionary', said Pfretschner, from the Tyrol. Similarly, Lasser, from Upper Austria, who added: 'I seek democracy in the rule of an enlightened majority, and therefore want members of the intelligentsia to be assured of seats in Parliament.' And Brestel, a Vienna intellectual: 'There is an aristocracy which you cannot destroy, the aristocracy of the *Intelligenz*,[4] and you had better recognise it.' Even the Czech Rieger, the only one to protest that peasant representatives should not be 'rejected outright', in defending the franchise and constituencies of 1848 excused the presence of a few peasants from Bohemia by their previous interest in the 'robot' problem. It was decided to assign in the larger towns one member to

---

[1] About Bach, see Friedjung, *Oesterreich von 1848 bis 1860*; the author had access to the Bach MSS.

[2] See Friedjung, 'Gegner der Bauernbefreiung in Oesterreich', in the *Vierteljahrschrift für Social- und Wirtschaftsgeschichte*, vol. i (1903). With Windischgrätz's dictum cf. the remark of an Austrian Pole, in W. N. Senior, *Journals in France and Italy, 1848–1852* (1871), under date of 20 May 1850 (vol. i, pp. 258–9): '. . . under the influence of Bach, the Minister of the Interior, whom Czarkowski calls a Communist, it [the Austrian Government] has abolished the *corvée*, and authorised the peasants to retain as owners the lands which they tenanted as occupiers.'

[3] See *Protokolle des Verfassungs-Ausschusses im Oesterreichischen Reichstag, 1848–49*. These were, however, notes, and not official, formally approved, minutes; see Odložilík, 'A Czech Plan for a Danubian Federation', in the *Journal of Central European Affairs*, Oct. 1941, vol. i, p. 261, n. 8.

[4] The word is ambiguous, and can be translated either as 'intelligence' or as 'intelligentsia': he obviously meant both, but in English there is, fortunately, no such confusion between the two.

15,000 inhabitants, but in the rural districts one to 60,000.[1] 'To whom do we owe it that we sit here?' asked the Czech Pinkas. 'To the Vienna and Prague risings.[2] What is our mainstay now? The towns only: for the peasants, freed from "robot", would not have moved had we been scattered to the winds.'[3] In fact, these middle-class intellectuals hoped that the peasant would take no further interest in politics.

On whom did they count to defend their newly conquered freedom? Not on the 'proletariate'. 'If proletarians were to vote in Parliamentary elections', declared Lasser, 'I would oppose the town representation.'[4] Fischhof, a Vienna Radical, though admitting that in a few districts of Bohemia and Silesia the social problem was acute, reassuringly pointed to the fact that the great majority of the population owned property, 'and small proprietors are the most conservative'. And Pinkas: 'Our proletariate, thank God, is not yet so dangerous: for its demonstrations in Vienna were a hothouse plant of the University.'[5]

The proletariate was defeated in Paris, the peasants were bought off in the Habsburg Monarchy. The social forces behind the revolution of 1848, disjointed and insufficient from the very outset, were thus practically eliminated. What re-

---

[1] Another proposal for achieving a drastic reduction in the peasant representation (which was not carried) was by creating large constituencies, as in France. It would not be easy for a peasant, argued Brestel, to be known in a wide district, 'and better-known men, of the educated class, would be returned'. Similarly the Czech Strobach: 'Then an obscure name will not carry, and I believe we shall have practically none but educated men in Parliament.' Also Ziemiałkowski favoured large constituencies, so as to exclude 'obscure men' (besides, he wished for a literacy test, which would have given a preponderance to the Polish gentry over the Polish peasants and the Ruthenes).

[2] Halter, of Salzburg, argued that as 'the towns conquered freedom, and with it the franchise', the seats conceded to the rural districts 'are a gracious gift, for which these are indebted to the towns'.

[3] These debates on parliamentary representation in the Constitutional Committee took place in Feb. 1849, and Pinkas's remark obviously refers to the fears that had been entertained of a dissolution of Parliament after the October Revolution in Vienna.

[4] Presumably he meant the four times greater representation of the towns.

[5] In the Vienna revolution university students played quite a leading part: the more immature politically a community, the younger, as a rule, its politicians—'paidocracy'.

One member of the Committee who was prepared to see 'proletarians' in Parliament, was Brestel: 'The election of two or three so-called proletarians . . . would be no misfortune; representation would promote respect for the laws and their stability.'

mained was the middle classes led by intellectuals, and their modern ideology with which they confronted the old established powers and interests. Foremost in that ideology was their demand for a share in the government of States to be remodelled in accordance with the national principle.

V

The basic conflict of 1848 was between two principles—of dynastic property in countries, and of national sovereignty: the one feudal in origin, historic in its growth and survival, deeply rooted, but difficult to defend in argument; the other grounded in reason and ideas, simple and convincing, but as unsuited to living organisms as chemically pure water. To the men of 1848 the dynastic principle stood for arbitrary rule and autocracy, that of popular sovereignty for human rights and national self-government: by a crude over-simplification the conflict presented itself to them as a fight between reason and unreason, between freedom and unfreedom. The British system of representative and responsible government, carried on through parliamentary institutions, seemed to them to secure in practice the basic maxims of the French Revolution; and they did not realize how deeply ingrained the proprietary principle is in the public life of this country, where even abuses tend to become freeholds with redeemable value, where to this day heredity enters into the choice of parliamentary representatives, and no basic distinction exists between private and public law. The proprietary claim of dynasties centres in the land, and works through it; popular sovereignty is primarily the claim of men considered apart from the land. The title of 'roi de France' stressed the territorial principle; 'roi des Français' transferred the emphasis to the human element, and paid tribute to the sovereignty of the people. The growth of urban agglomerations and of an urban civilization stimulates the rise of a non-territorial ideology, but unless there be a complete return to the conditions of the horde, the basic element of territory cannot be eliminated: there is no escape from the interplay between groups of men and tracts of land, which forms the essence of history.

In central Europe the principle of dynastic property in countries found its most striking expression in the Habsburg Monarchy, and its caricature in the German pygmy States. Neither offered the basis for a sovereign national State. In the Habsburg Monarchy its emergence was precluded by the diversity of populations which, 'through lack of a fellow feeling', could not 'unite in maintaining their liberties or in forming a paramount public opinion'.[1] The bond of union between them was primarily dynastic—Schuselka, one of the leaders of the Left in the Frankfort Parliament, thus descanted upon it in 1847: '. . . the Austrian peoples . . . in their happy land, welded through the historically valid hereditary right of the House of Habsburg-Lorraine into a Great Power of the first order, this is Austria!'[2] There, even after 1848, the dynastic principle, pure and simple, was kept alive for another seventy years: bolstered up at various times by particular national interests, but at no time reinforced by a feeling of community between the component parts; and to the very end the provinces of Austria continued to bear the expressive designation of *Kronländer* (Crownlands).[3] The pygmy States, on the other hand, lacked the substance of national organisms. When the Pre-Parliament fixed the normal constituency for the Frankfort Parliament at 50,000 inhabitants, the charitable proviso was added that any State which did not attain to that size should form, none the less, a self-contained constituency.[4] And in some cases such a tiny territory consisted of a dozen fragments. These were but large feudal estates which, paradoxically, had come to be endowed with the courtesy standing of sovereign States.[5] From the Habsburg Monarchy at the top, and the pygmy States at the bottom, the principle of dynastic property

[1] J. S. Mill, in an article on 'The French Revolution and its Assailants', in the *Westminster Review* for Apr. 1849, writing about the difficulty of forcing unwilling nations into political community.

[2] *Oesterreichische Vor- und Rückschritte* (1847), p. 5. I quote this piece of dynastic bombast because it comes from a member of the Left. In reality Schuselka was not even an honest Great-Austrian, but much rather a Bohemian Pan-German. In the same book (pp. 270–95) he urges the giving up of Galicia so as to lighten 'the Slav burden of Austria' and to secure a better preponderance for the Germans over the other Slavs. The Czechs, according to him, must 'remain connected with Germany' and will probably 'be absorbed completely in the German element'.

[3] The Constitutional Committee of the Austrian Parliament at Kremsier proposed to change their name to *Reichsländer*, to avoid the feudal connotation; see *Protokolle des Verfassungs-Ausschusses im Oesterreichischen Reichstag, 1848–49*, pp. 117–18.

[4] There were, in 1819, twelve such States with less than 50,000 inhabitants in the Federation, seven with a population of 50,000–100,000, ten with 100,000–500,000, and only nine with more than half a million (see 'Matrikel des deutschen Bundes', in *Verhandlungen des deutschen Parlaments. Offizielle Ausgabe. Zweite Lieferung*, 1848, pp. 509–10).

[5] The difference between the proprietary, dynastic German States and

in countries seemed to colour off on to all Germany and Italy, and through the great syndicate of German dynasties, on to most of the European Continent. In the Habsburg interest the dynastic principle was consciously fostered by Metternich: and therefore the struggle for the principle of national sovereignty— for the unification of Germany and Italy, and the rise of the smaller nationalities in the European Middle-East—became, first and foremost, a fight against the Habsburg Monarchy. Hübner, Austrian Ambassador in Paris, records having said to Napoleon III on 15 May 1858: 'Every Power, Sire . . . has a moral basis from which it cannot depart unpunished. . . . Austria has for principle the respect due to the imprescriptible rights of sovereigns, and non-recognition of the claim of nationalities to set up as political States.'[1]

The right to self-government and the right to self-determination are corollaries of the principle of national sovereignty. Because both run counter to that of dynastic property in countries, they were looked upon as cognate causes favouring each other. But constitutional development is based on States within their existing frontiers: it is therefore apt to foster organic unity even where the State is non-national and artificial in origin, and thus to work against a reallocation, or a union, of territories in accordance with language, which continental nationalisms have adopted for basis of common citizenship. Self-determination, on the other hand, contests frontiers, negates

modern national States was implicitly acknowledged in the different formulas adopted for territorial cessions to these two types in the Treaty of Westphalia of 1648, and in the *Reichsdeputationshauptschluss* of 1803: in the case of the small German States it shows *ein patrimonial-privatrechtliches Gepräge*. In the Treaty of Osnabrück, Bremen and Verden, though held 'a caesarea majestate et imperio' (of Germany), were ceded 'reginae et futuris ejus heredibus ac successoribus, regibus regnoque Sueciae'; while in cessions, for instance, to Brandenburg, Mecklenburg, or Hesse, only the princes and their heirs were mentioned, not their principalities (see H. O. Meissner, *Die Lehre vom monarchischen Prinzip*, in the *Untersuchungen zur deutschen Staats- und Rechtsgeschichte*, vol. cxxii (1913), pp. 134–5 n., and H. Preuss, *Gemeinde, Staat, Reich als Gebietskörperschaften*, p. 355).

In the Carlsbad Conference of Aug. 1819, and in the Vienna Conferences (Nov. 1819 to May 1820), Metternich made great play with Art. 13 of the Federal Act of 1815: 'In all States of the [German] Confederation there shall be a constitution based on Estates' (*eine landständische Verfassung*). He thought assemblies based on Estates compatible with the proprietary right of dynasties, but not representative assemblies chosen on the principle of numbers, no matter by what franchise; these he considered to imply popular sovereignty (see Meissner, op. cit.).

[1] *Neuf ans de souvenirs d'un ambassadeur d'Autriche à Paris*, vol. ii (1904), p. 164.

the existing State and its inner development, and by civil and international strife is apt to stultify constitutional growth. In 1848 the vices of governments were known and the virtues of 'free peoples' were extolled, the diplomacy of courts was charged with having set nations against each other, and 'dynastic ambitions' were singled out as the cause of wars. On the morning of 13 March 1848, Dr. Adolf Fischhof, a young Jewish physician, thus addressed the crowd in the Inner Court of the Landhaus: 'Hitherto an ill-advised system of government has kept the peoples of Austria apart. They must now fraternally find each other. . . .' What could not be achieved by 'a vigorous co-operation in the tasks of State' between Germans, Slavs, Magyars, and Italians!—'you cannot doubt that Austria's position in Europe would be remarkable'. He concluded with cheers for 'Austria and her Glorious Future', for the 'United Peoples of Austria', and for 'Liberty'.[1] Could he have repeated that speech a year later? The sovereignty of the people merely substitutes the proprietary claims of nations for those of princes, because States are still based on territories and not on 'sovereign' hordes: and the conflicts grow fiercer.

VI

The first moves in the revolution naturally took existing States for their starting-point: constitutional freedoms were demanded, liberal governments were set up, representative assemblies were conceded: and thus new vested political interests were developed in States which had hitherto been merely dynastic creations and inheritances. With that purpose in view even before 1848 some German States, more particularly in the south, had favoured parliamentary development; on the outbreak of the revolution 'Prussia and a number of Federal States', especially among those dependent on her, tried, with noticeable haste, in assemblies of their own to create counterweights to the Frankfort Parliament'.[2] In the past the German people

---

[1] See R. Charmatz, *Adolf Fischhof* (1910), pp. 20–1. Charmatz, himself a Jew, remarks about Fischhof: 'He was the first German to make a sensible treatment of nationalities the central theme of his discourse' (p. 25). Fischhof's father was a Moravian Jew settled in Budapest, his mother an Hungarian Jewess, he himself was born and educated in Hungary, and only came to Vienna to study at the University, some thirteen years before the revolution. 'Germans' of that description have been tolerant and reasonable, and are made to pay for it.

[2] Valentin, op. cit., vol. ii, p. 42.

'had produced too many princes, too many noblemen, too many cities. . . . Now, side by side with the Frankfort Parliament, there was the Austrian Reichstag, the Prussian National Assembly, and a host of parliaments in the small States (*der Vielparlamentarismus der Kleinstaaterei*).'[1] The Austrian Germans enthusiastically supported the idea of a united Greater Germany and took a leading part in the Frankfort National Parliament, but saw nothing incompatible in the simultaneous deliberations of the Austrian Constituent Assembly: in Frankfort they tried to exercise national sovereignty joined in one body politic with Prussians, Bavarians, Hessians, &c., and in Vienna in another, joined with Czechs, Poles, Ruthenes, Italians, &c. (and they finished by voting for themselves in the two Parliaments two different sets of 'fundamental rights'—*Grundrechte*). Frederick William IV declared on 21 March: 'Henceforth Prussia merges into Germany';[2] but when the Prussian Constituent Assembly met on 22 May, the King's Speech explained that 'the internal conditions in Prussia did not permit awaiting the outcome of the Frankfort Parliament, though German unity remained the unalterable goal'.[3] Here was an assembly, gathered in the capital of a living State and legislating for more than one-third of the population represented at Frankfort[4]—a powerful political reality without logical foundation competing against an idea as yet lacking substance, but strongly upheld by all educated Germans.

National ideas seeking embodiment must start by making

[1] Valentin, op. cit., vol. ii, p. 2.

[2] *Preussen geht fortan in Deutschland auf.* 'It is feared that you intend merging all German Governments into the Prussian', wrote to him on 24 March, his brother-in-law and close friend, Frederick Augustus II of Saxony (see K. Haenchen, *Revolutionsbriefe, 1848, Ungedrucktes aus dem Nachlass König Friedrich Wilhelms IV von Preussen*, 1930, p. 56).

[3] Valentin, op. cit., vol. ii, p. 42.

[4] The way in which constitutional growth was apt to stimulate State patriotism can be seen, for instance, in the case of the Rhinelander, David Hansemann, one of the early champions of German unity, and from Mar. to Sept. 1848 Prussian Minister of Finance. In Oct. 1848 he published a pamphlet, *Die deutsche Verfassungsfrage*, critical of attempts to found, in spite of existing States, a unitary German constitutional monarchy based on direct popular sovereignty: 'were it possible—which is doubtful—to destroy completely the separate life of Prussia, it would be a mistake to do so, for this would weaken, and not strengthen, Germany' (p. 17). The pamphlet is not dated, but on p. 5 he speaks of the Frankfort Assembly and 'its five months' experience', and in a later pamphlet *Das preussische und deutsche Verfassungswerk* (1850), p. 131, he refers to the other as written in Oct. 1848.

State organisms their basis, or at least by having recourse to the memories of such organisms; but in doing so, they pass from the nation as a collection of men to the territory, enter the thickets of historical tradition and heritage, and lose their logical simplicity and cogency—the less there was in 1848 (or in 1918) of an existing substructure on which to build a national State, the more there was of antiquarian ferreting.

Still, even among the submerged or partitioned nations, with whom the cause of national revival or reunion was the alpha and omega of politics, the revolution of 1848 started with demands for political freedom and for linguistic rights within existing territorial divisions, most often historic provinces. Thus the Prague petition of 11–12 March was of a constitutional and provincial rather than of a Czech national character, and the Germans joined in it, the two nations joyfully fraternizing. But by the end of the month, the Czechs having clearly formulated their national programme of a self-governing union of the three Czech provinces of Bohemia, Moravia, and Austrian Silesia, and their claim to equality with the Germans having assumed concrete forms, the 'Sudeten' Germans were in full hue and cry against them.

Similarly in Posnania the Poles and Germans tried at first to fraternize in 'freedom', and the Posnanian delegates, who saw Frederick William IV on 23 March, were subsequently blamed by their Polish countrymen for having restricted their demands too much to mere provincial affairs.[1] But the request made by the Germans of Poznań for representation on the Polish Committee was refused;[2] and by the end of the month,

---

[1] See e.g. J. Moraczewski, *Wypadki poznańskie z r. 1848 (The Posnanian Events of 1848)* (1850); the author was one of the leaders of the Posnanian Poles. J. Feldman, in his book *Sprawa polska w r. 1848 (The Polish Question in 1848)* (1933) tries, but not altogether convincingly, to rebut that contention. An account of the audience with the King, compiled from German reports, is printed in an appendix to the pamphlet, *Im Polen-Aufruhr, 1846–48. Aus den Papieren eines Landrats.* For the text of the petition submitted to the King, see K. Rakowski, *Powstanie poznańskie w 1848 roku (The Posnanian Revolution in 1848)* (1900), Appendix, pp. 15–16.

[2] See Kohte, op. cit., p. 22, and K. Rakowski, op. cit., pp. 86–7; the Polish answer of 23 Mar. (which was, to say the least, evasive) is printed in R. Hepke, *Die polnische Erhebung und die deutsche Gegenbewegung in Posen im Frühling 1848* (1848), p. 38: '. . . as the activities of the Polish National Committee are not confined to the Grand Duchy [Posnania], but have for their aim the independence of the whole of Poland . . . the Committee do not feel authorised . . . to give an immediate and definite reply to your question "whether the German element of this town will receive representation on the National

the national conflict between Poles and Germans was in full blast.

The Lvov petition of 18 March, drafted by two men who henceforth stood in the forefront of Galician politics,[1] dealt exclusively with provincial problems; it pressed the claims of the Polish language in schools and offices, demanded an autonomous administration staffed by natives, a representative Diet, &c., but did not raise the wider problem of Poland's resurrection. Moreover, the petition dealing with a province in which the Poles formed less than half the population,[2] but practically the whole of the educated classes, forgot to mention the existence and rights of the other nationality, the Ruthenes. After the delegation who were taking the petition to Vienna had been joined by representatives from Cracow (only since 1846 incorporated in Galicia), a new petition was drafted[3] of a wider, Polish national, character, and also conceding elementary schools 'in the local language'—thus Ruthene was included without being named. The Ruthenes, on their part, pressed the demand for a division of Galicia into two provinces in accordance with nationality, and the Poles, who were so insistent in urging their own national claims, began to resort to every sophistry and distortion in order to defeat those of the Ruthenes.[4]

The 'provincial' character of the original Polish resolutions, both in Posnania and in Galicia, was subsequently used at Frankfort as an argument against wider Polish national claims.[5]

Committee"; the decision must much rather be left to the new Government now to be formed.' The Germans thereupon formed a committee of their own.

[1] Smolka and Ziemiałkowski, who were subsequently the two Polish representatives on the Constitutional Committee of the Austrian Parliament 1848–9. Smolka was Vice-President of that Parliament Sept.–Nov. 1848, and its President Nov.–Dec. 1848, and Jan.–Mar. 1849; and again President of the Austrian Parliament 1881–93. Ziemiałkowski was Minister for Galicia 1873–88. The third draftsman, Heffern, was of minor importance.

[2] See Ostaszewski-Barański, op. cit., p. 75; he puts the number of Roman Catholics in Galicia in 1848 at 2,258,933; of Greek Catholics at 2,303,222; and of Jews at 328,026. Till the end of the century, when the Poles started falsifying Galician language statistics, the numbers of the Ruthene-speaking population invariably exceeded that of Greek Catholics.

[3] See Ziemiałkowski, op. cit., part ii, p. 16.

[4] For the Polish attitude towards the Ruthenes and their demands in 1848, see protocols of Polish-Ruthene Section of the Prague Slav Congress published by W. T. Wisłocki, *Kongres Słowiański w r. 1848 i sprawa polska*, and Łoziński, *Agenor hr. Gołuchowski*, pp. 126–62.

[5] See, for instance, debate on Poland in the Committee of Fifty, 26 Apr.

VII

In the interplay between constitutional and national movements on the European Continent, which opens in 1848, it is
the latter that win: and they cut across into the international
arena. A constitutional régime is secure when its ways have
become engrained in the habits and instinctive reactions—*dans
les mœurs*—of the political nation: it safeguards civilized life,
but it presupposes agreement and stability as much as it secures
them; and it can hardly be expected to build up, recast, or
dissect the body·in which it resides. (Hence the talk about
'missed opportunities' of uniting Germany by 'Parliamentary
action' lacks substance.) States are not created or destroyed,
and frontiers redrawn or obliterated, by argument and majority
votes; nations are freed, united, or broken by blood and iron,
and not by a generous application of liberty and tomato-sauce;
violence is the instrument of national movements. Mass violence
takes two forms, denoted as revolution and war; and there is
close interaction between the two—they shatter political struc-
tures, and open the way for each other. In 1848 the subversive
social forces were not equal to the task, and war had to come
first: hence the bellicose ardours of the social revolutionaries, and the prudent pacificism of the Conservatives—for
once both sides understood their business (better, indeed, than
many historians who have written about it since). The national
revolutionaries, recruited mainly from the middle classes
or the petty gentry, and, most of all, from the intellectuals,
could not become effective except by laying hold of governments and armies: as in Piedmont and Hungary. But these
were small States, the one hampered by hesitations and the
other beset with difficulties, which still further reduced their
strength, while Prussia's action in Slesvig-Holstein was less than
half-hearted. Throughout 1848 the ultimate control of the
state-machine, and still more of the armies of the Great Powers
on the European Continent, remained with the Conservatives;
and it is this which preserved peace in Europe. The 'Revolution
of the Intellectuals' exhausted itself without achieving concrete
results: it left its imprint only in the realm of ideas.

1848, *Verhandlungen des deutschen Parlaments*, Offizielle Ausgabe. Zweite
Lieferung (1848). Also General W. von Willisen, a friend of the Poles who
was in touch with their deputation, says that its claims were of a purely
provincial character ('sie hatten nur rein Provinzielles zu bitten'); see
Willisen, *Akten und Bemerkungen über meine Sendung nach dem Grossherzogtum
Posen im Frühjahr 1848* (1850), p. 3.

C

In its initial stage it looked to Britain and her parliamentary
Government for patterns; and Englishmen, conscious of the
excellence of their constitutional system and ascribing to it
universal applicability, responded by taking a benevolent,
fatherly, interest in these endeavours. They also sympathized
with national aspirations, if respectable and 'legitimate';[1] but
few there were who would have dissented from Palmerston's
pronouncement that peace was 'the first object, to the attain-
ment of which the efforts of enlightened statesmen ought to
be directed'.[2] As yet the conflict between constitutional development and national movements was not patent: and its unfolding
in 1848 could be written in terms of British disillusionment and
disgust. Lord Minto had a foretaste of it when in 1847-8 he went
out to Italy with a roving commission, and set to work to teach
rulers how to carry on constitutional government, and liberal
leaders how to conduct an opposition; failing in either task, he
bitterly concluded that 'rogues and fools and cowards form the
whole stock-in-trade of this country in the article of public
men'. And after the *annus mirabilis* had run its course, early
in 1849, Lord Brougham wrote in his magniloquent manner:
'I must . . . lift up my voice against that new speculation in the
rights of independent States, the security of neighbouring
governments, and indeed the happiness of all nations . . . termed
"Nationality", adopted as a kind of rule for the distribution of
dominion.'[3] While rebutting some of Brougham's indictments
of the revolution, John Stuart Mill sadly reflected on the feelings
which make men indifferent to the rights and interests 'of any
portion of the human species, save that which is called by the
same name and speaks the same language as themselves. These
feelings are characteristic of barbarians.' Now it was seen 'that
in the backward parts of Europe and even (where better things
might have been expected) in Germany, the sentiment of
nationality so far outweighs the love of liberty that the people
are willing to abet their rulers in crushing the liberty and independence of any people not of their race and language'.[4]

---

[1] That is, of nations whose representatives were fit to frequent London
society, or whose countries were attractive to British tourists.

[2] See A. J. P. Taylor, *The Italian Problem in European Diplomacy, 1847–49*
(1934), p. 72.

[3] See *Letter to the Marquess of Lansdowne, Lord President of the Council*, p. 126.

[4] See article on 'The French Revolution and its Assailants', in the *Westminster Review* for Apr. 1849. Meyendorff, himself a German but of the
ancien régime, at an early date discerned the nature and significance of the
German national movement. He wrote to Nesselrode on 29 Mar.: 'I have

Lastly, W. N. Senior, in 1850: 'This barbarous feeling of nationality . . . has become the curse of Europe.'[1]

Thus in the *Völkerfrühling*[2], 'nationality', the passionate creed of the intellectuals, invades the politics of central and east-central Europe, and with 1848 starts the Great European War of every nation against its neighbours. But this is a theme so massive in its core and so vast in its ramifications that not even a summary can be attempted in this paper. I shall limit myself to certain international developments during the first months of the revolution, and to the early manifestations of aggressive nationalisms, especially of German nationalism which derives from the much belauded Frankfort Parliament rather than from Bismarck and 'Prussianism'; and in examining the relation of these German 'Liberals', in reality forerunners of Hitler, to the Poles and Czechs, and also of the Poles to the other Slavs, I shall be discussing problems which ninety years later, in 1938–9, were to become once more a touchstone of German mentality, and a decisive element in East-European politics. An analysis of other problems in 1848—those of German unity, of the Habsburg Monarchy, of the Hungarian National State, of the 'subject nationalities', of Italy, of parliamentary assemblies, &c., I must leave to further essays.[3]

VIII

In February 1848, in Paris, political passions devoid of real contents had evoked revolutionary phantoms: fevered nerves and hearts grown cold responded to an overtowering past by a routine of excitement. How far would reverberations and memories carry France in the sphere of international action?

put a Danish Minister, called Lehmann, in touch with Sir Stratford Canning, so that England should see how hostile national Germany is to all other nationalities, and how it threatens the peace of Europe which England desires to preserve' (op. cit., vol. ii, pp. 58–9).

[1] See *Journals in France and Italy, 1848–52*, vol. i, p. 262, under date 20 May 1850.

[2] 'The springtime of nations': the Germans wax sentimental about 'March 1848', which to them is the *Wonnemond* of history; and they have managed to make other nations believe that there was something specially noble and precious and liberal-minded about the collectivity of Germans at that time, and about their performance—one of the legends of history.

[3] In the lecture as delivered to the British Academy I touched on some of these problems, but having much more fully developed and documented the part here comprised, I could not include these other major themes without exceeding by far the limits of an essay.

How much of the drama would be restaged? France was not alone in remembering 1792: and the Great Powers, having learnt their lesson, steered clear of war.

In French home politics, 1848 continued the unfinished story of 1830—'En 1830, nous nous sommes fort hâtés, nous voici obligés, en 1848, de recommencer';[1] in foreign affairs, it merely supplied a revised edition. Once more the traditional revolutionary cries were heard, but there was no *élan*, no sacrificial zeal—as in 1830 'the revolutionary spirit still declaimed and agitated the masses, but did not fire them any longer with an ardent and devoted eagerness'. 'The revolutionary party . . . thought war inevitable for France and necessary for itself, and, blindly assuming the inheritance both of the Convention and the Empire, raised the double standard of propaganda and conquest: yet expected to find for its enterprise allies in Europe.'[2] But the masses—'those millions which make no noise but are France'[3]—would not have marched unless France were attacked.

War presaged revolutionary violence and a Caesarian dictatorship: contingencies repugnant to the middle classes and their intellectual leaders. They desired peace and prosperity, facilities for work and study, freedom and the pleasures of a brilliant intellectual life, an existence rendered glorious by pride of place: by the consciousness of France's intellectual, moral, and political primacy in Europe. This was not a German militarism or *Wille zur Macht*, but a perplexing mixture of *hubris* and idealism. 'The permanent rôle of France is . . . to promote civilisation and liberal ideas, and to protect the independence of small States'[4] wrote d'Haussonville in 1850. And again: 'It has always been the fate of France by her power to arouse anxiety among her neighbours . . . the jealousy of Europe is our honour and our danger. Shame to us if we cease to merit that honour or recoil from that danger!'[5] Crémieux, a member of the Provisional Government of February, in December 1848 supported Louis-Napoleon for the Presidency as 'the clearest protest against the Treaties of 1815, the most complete break

[1] Crémieux in the French Parliament on 24 Feb. 1848.

[2] Guizot, *Mémoires*, vol. ii, p. 85 and p. 80. These two passages refer to the early days of the July Monarchy, but, written in the fifties, seem to reflect 1848.

[3] Ibid., vol. iii, p. 12.

[4] *Histoire de la politique extérieure du gouvernement français, 1830–1848* (1850), pp. x–xi.

[5] Ibid., p. 15.

with that anti-national era which sullies our history'.[1] Circourt, a Legitimist, writes of 1848: 'France at that time seemed invested with the privilege, great and dangerous, to feel, to think, to speak, and to act in the name of humanity.'[2] With this belief the French democrats of 1848 combined a naive pacifism imbued with romantic sensibility—they had faith in the *sympathie pacifique des peuples*.[3] France sang the 'Marseillaise' and talked peace. Lamartine managed to voice and blend these two emotions. He was a poet and an orator, and vain, but a sincere pacifist;[4] and in his foreign policy he showed a common sense in which otherwise he was frequently deficient.[5] On 27 February, he wrote in a circular to the foreign ambassadors in Paris:[6]

The Republican form of the new Government has not altered the place of France in Europe, nor her loyal and sincere disposition to maintain friendly relations with all Powers which, like herself, desire the independence of nations and the peace of the world.

And in his 'Manifesto to the Powers' on 4 March (a tirade of well over 2,500 words)[7]:

The proclamation of the French Republic is not directed against

[1] *La Révolution de 1848. Bulletin de la Société d'Histoire de la Révolution de 1848*, vol. xxi, Dec. 1924, p. 266. This explanation is given in a letter to his nephew, Aimé Lyon, dated 7 Mar. 1849.

[2] *Souvenirs d'une mission à Berlin en 1848*, vol. i, p. 88.

[3] See Laurin, 'Un précurseur de la Société des Nations', in *La Révolution de 1848. Bulletin* &c., vol. xxi, July–August 1924.

[4] When in the debate on the Paris fortifications in Aug. 1845 Thiers, both statesman and *brouillon*, remarked: 'Nous sommes toujours en 1792, et l'Europe nous menace toujours', Lamartine replied: 'Cinquante ans ont passé depuis 1792, et personne ne menace la France . . .' (see Daniel Halévy, *Le Courrier de M. Thiers*, 1921, p. 185). In a speech delivered at Macon, in the autumn of 1847, Lamartine said about the July Monarchy: 'La paix sera dans l'avenir, selon moi, la glorieuse amnistie de ce gouvernement contre ses autres erreurs' (see his *Histoire de la Révolution de 1848*, vol. i, p. 35).

[5] Absent from Lamartine's cradle, says Sainte-Beuve, was 'la fée du bons sens et du sens réel' (see Essay on Lamartine's *Confidences* in *Causeries de Lundi*, vol. i, 8 Oct. 1849). No need to resort to Lamartine's *Confidences* for evidence—witness the self-lyricism of his *Histoire de la Révolution de 1848*. For instance: 'il avait beaucoup conversé avec la nature, avec les livres, avec son cœur, avec ses pensées (vol. i, p. 74): about his journey to the East: 'On était parti homme, on revient philosophe' (p. 76); or this self-portrait: 'Lamartine avait été créé religieux, comme l'air a été créé transparent. Le sentiment de Dieu était tellement indivisible de son âme, qu'il était impossible de distinguer en lui la politique de la religion' (pp. 81–2).

[6] See Lamartine, *Trois mois au pouvoir* (1848), p. 68.

[7] Ibid., pp. 69–78. Lamartine had 'une phraséologie abondante et monotone', and found it convenient 'de couronner sa politique par des idylles' (Sainte-Beuve).

any other form of Government. . . . Monarchy and Republic are not . . . absolute principles in deadly conflict; they can face each other with mutual understanding and respect. . . .

The French Republic will not start war against anyone. The men who now govern France think: Happy is France if war is declared on her, and she is constrained to acquire strength and glory, despite her moderation! But terrible would be her responsibility were she to declare war unprovoked! . . .

The Treaties of 1815 legally no longer exist in the eyes of the French Republic; still, their territorial clauses are a fact admitted by her as basis and starting point in relations with other nations . . . this emancipation of the Republic from the Treaties of 1815 is in no way irreconcilable with the tranquillity of Europe.

But we declare that if the hour for the resurrection of some oppressed nations . . . should seem to us to have struck in the decrees of Providence; if Switzerland, our faithful ally were . . . menaced; if the independent States of Italy were invaded; if limits or obstacles were placed to their internal transformation; if the right to federate were forcibly denied to them . . . the French Republic would feel entitled to take up arms in defence of these legitimate movements. . . .

The Republic, at birth, pronounced . . . the three words, *Liberté, Égalité, Fraternité*. . . . If Europe is wise and just, each of them signifies *peace.*

In short: no ideological wars, no republican propaganda, no programme of conquest; a reservation is made against foreign intervention in the *pays limitrophes* (such as was made by Sebastiani and Casimir Périer in 1830–1); the fate of Poland (a country not mentioned by name) is left to the decrees of Providence (as interpreted by France).[1] There was enough verbiage to satisfy the public at home, and enough sense to reassure European statesmen. 'If the Powers of Europe wished

---

[1] Lamartine said to a Polish deputation: 'The Republic . . . said, thinking of you: The day when the providential hour will seem to us to have struck for the resurrection of a nation unjustly wiped off the map, we shall fly to its help. But we have reserved the right of France to appraise the hour, the moment, the justice, the cause, and the means whereby it suits us to intervene' (*Trois mois au pouvoir*, p. 135; the address is printed under 19 Mar. 1848, and reproduced without date in Lamartine's *Histoire de la Révolution de 1848*, vol. ii, pp. 259–66; but its correct date is 26 Mar.—see official *Moniteur* of 27 Mar., p. 695). Guizot, when criticizing in his *Mémoires* (vol. ii, p. 84, published in 1859) the foreign policy of the Left in the early 30's, undoubtedly had also Lamartine's circular in mind: 'They did not mean to brush aside or break those treaties, for they wanted peace; but they wished both to respect and to denounce them, and to utter threats without acting; an attitude maladroit and undignified, for their words aroused suspicions abroad which their conduct endeavoured to allay.'

to make war against France, there are in that circular abundant materials wherewith to pick a quarrel with her', wrote Palmerston to the British Ambassador in Paris; but if they are desirous of maintaining peace, its substance is in the circular, 'although somewhat clothed in the garb of defiance'.[1]

This, moreover, Lamartine tried to explain away in advance by means of confidential messages. On 3 March he spoke to Normanby about 'the feeling which had existed for the last thirty years in France upon the subject of the Treaties of 1815, and the humiliation of which they had been considered as the constant record; he should have wished to have said nothing whatever about them, but this seemed impossible'—and he explained the way in which he proposed to deal with the subject.[2] Even before addressing himself to Normanby, Lamartine forewarned the Duke of Wellington: 'Le Gouvernement Provisoire . . . fera une déclaration énergique aux nations de l'Europe, mais le Duc de Wellington en comprendra le vrai sens.'[3] (Republicans had talked of 'the malady of 1815' and 'the poignant memories of Waterloo': now to pick out the Duke of all men for recipient of such a message—how truly romantic!) And on 5 March Lamartine instructed Circourt to reassure the King of Prussia: 'In Paris we have successfully stood between anarchy and order. . . . With the same energy, we now wish to stand between war and Europe.'[4]

[1] Lord Palmerston to Lord Normanby (draft), P.R.O., F.O., 27/804, No. 132; in the heading the draft bears the date of 6 Mar. 1848, but against Palmerston's initial that of 7 Mar. is added.

[2] Normanby to Palmerston, F.O., 27/804, No. 118.

[3] The Duke received this on 2 Mar. through his nephew, J. Wellesley, in 'a communication made to him for me by M. de Lamartine, which he wrote down in M. de Lamartine's presence, and read to him'. The import of the memorandum, which the Duke was asked to lay before Her Majesty's servants, was the wish for an alliance with Great Britain; see Spencer Walpole, *The Life of Lord John Russell* (1889), vol. ii, p. 32. The exchange of messages with the Duke is mentioned in Lamartine's *Histoire de la Révolution de 1848* (vol. ii, p. 32), in general terms and with a clever shifting of emphasis: while his message was *empressé* and the Duke's reply non-committal, Lamartine, though admitting that the initiative had been his, veils its character and makes the most of the Duke's answer—'the first impression of England expressed through her first citizen'.

[4] Circourt, op. cit., vol. i, p. 80. Lamartine was half-inclined to look upon Prussia as a liberal, semi-constitutional State; for the importance which he ascribed to Prussia, and a romantic discourse on 'the heart of the King', see his *Histoire de la Révolution de 1848*, vol. ii, pp. 175-9. But the message to Wellington classes Frederick William with Metternich and Tsar Nicholas: the Provisional Government 'wants to defend the free nations

Louis-Philippe and Guizot could hardly have improved on this language.[1]

That the July Monarchy was nowhere cherished or esteemed was an initial safeguard against the blunder of 1792. John Russell, voicing the resentment still felt in London over the Spanish marriages, wrote to the Queen on 15 April:

The King of the French has brought upon his own family, upon France, and upon Europe, a great calamity. A moderate and constitutional Government at home, coupled with an abstinence from ambitious projects for his family abroad, might have laid the foundations of permanent peace, order, and freedom in Europe. Selfishness and cunning have destroyed that which honesty and wisdom might have maintained.[2]

Similarly, though for different reasons, the votaries of Legitimism derived moral comfort from the downfall of the July Monarchy. 'Who would not recognise the avenging hand of the King of Kings in all this?' wrote Frederick William IV to Queen Victoria on 28 February.[3] And Tsar Nicholas to Frederick William, on 7 March: 'Louis-Philippe loses his usurped throne. . . . Thus the hand of God is clearly seen. . . .'[4] 'What lessons for the world!' cogitated Metternich.

'We have no intention whatever', declared Lord John Russell on 28 February, 'to interfere with the form of government which the French nation may choose to adopt, or in any way to meddle with the affairs of that country.'[5] Even more: Great Britain meant to restrain Europe from doing so, provided France refrained from attacking Europe.[6] Britain's programme was thus summarized, on 27 February, by the Prussian Ambassador, Baron von Bunsen:[7]

against aggression from the Northern Courts, and hopes to find support in England'.

[1] Lamartine once said that 'though no one was a more determined advocate of the *status quo* and a more ardent lover of peace, he could not earn the character of the Guizot of the Republic' (see Normanby's dispatch of 1 May 1848, in Alan J. P. Taylor's *The Italian Problem in European Diplomacy, 1847–1849*, p. 95, n. 3). So he himself noted the resemblance, be it merely in a disclaimer.

[2] *The Letters of Queen Victoria, 1837–1861*, vol. ii, pp. 169–70.

[3] Ibid., p. 152.

[4] See Schiemann, *Geschichte Russlands under Kaiser Nikolaus I*, vol. iv (1919), p. 139.   [5] *Hansard*, vol. xcvi, c. 1389.

[6] Palmerston to Clarendon, 9 Mar. 1848: see E. Ashley, *Life of Lord Palmerston, 1846–1865* (1876), vol. i, p. 86.

[7] In a dispatch to Frederick William IV: see H. C. F. Bell, *Lord Palmerston* (1936), vol. i, p. 426.

Whatever happens, no offensive war against France, still less a war of principles; no . . . alliance . . . to such an end, but an agreement with the other Powers for the defence of the *status quo* against unprovoked attacks on the part of France. . . .

Nor had the continental rulers, though deeply apprehensive of French Republican aggression, any marked desire to plunge into preventive action. Frederick William, writing to Queen Victoria on 27 February, pleaded for resorting not to arms, but to 'the power of united speech': France should be told that no encroachment was intended, but that to 'the first breach of the peace', the Great Powers would react with their united forces.[1] To Bunsen he described this letter as his *credo*. 'My prayer to God, my longing and wishes, are for peace in Europe.'[2] Tsar Nicholas urged 'energetic resistance to the progress of anarchy which threatens the whole of Europe':[3] impressive forces should be assembled for defence. But even he meant to remain an onlooker of the 'new political experiment' and of the consequent 'work of disorganisation, so long as it does not exceed the frontiers of France'.[4] Metternich wrote on 7 March, in his draft for a Four-Power Declaration: 'The Courts do not regard themselves as called upon to interfere in questions which only concern the internal affairs of France'; he wished, however, to recreate the Grand Alliance and to wring from France an acknowledgement of the Treaty Settlement of 1815.[5] But Palmerston was opposed to exacting any such 'abstract and theoretical acknowledgment',[6] and would not engage in any great, or futile, 'political demonstration which might be misrepresented by the war party in France as an indication of intended attack, and would probably compel the Provisional Government to march troops and form armies. . . .'[7]

[1] *The Letters of Queen Victoria*, vol. ii, p. 151.

[2] See letter of 9 Mar. 1848, *Aus dem Briefwechsel Friedrich Wilhelms IV mit Bunsen*, edited by Leopold von Ranke (1873), pp. 178–81.

[3] In an official note published in the *Journal de St. Pétersbourg*; see Vicomte de Guichen, *Les grandes questions européennes et la diplomatie des puissances sous la Seconde République Française* (1925), vol. i, p. 58; the date is not clearly indicated, but seems to be 5 Mar.

[4] See letter from Nicholas I to Frederick William IV, 7 Mar. (N.S.), Schiemann, op. cit., vol. iv, pp. 139–40, and from Count Nesselrode, the Russian Chancellor, to Baron von Brunow, 12 Mar. (N.S.), Guichen, op. cit., vol. i, p. 60.

[5] See Metternich's *Mémoires* (1883), vol. vii, pp. 598–9.

[6] Palmerston to Normanby, 6–7 Mar., F.O., 27/804, No. 132.

[7] See Palmerston's dispatch to Normanby, 4 Mar. 1848; Taylor, op. cit., p. 74, n. 1.

D'Haussonville's description of Tsar Nicholas's attitude in
1830 applies also to 1848: 'Much anger . . . much ill-will towards
the French Government. As for a precise plan, he had none
either for himself or for the others.'[1] And before a month had
passed, revolution had engulfed central Europe. The war which
would have made France 'happy' by forcing her 'to acquire
strength and glory' (and might have averted the June Days) was
not declared on her: and the storm-centre moved eastward.

IX

Now it was a question of the attitude not of Courts only, but
of peoples, and of their interaction. German Liberals and
Radicals acknowledged the debt owing to the French Revolution, and professed reverence for the French champions of
human rights and freedom: but they could not overlook the
nexus between French revolutionary propaganda and demands
for the 'natural frontiers'. When in 1840 France threatened to
play off revolution against the Governments of Europe, and
talked of 'carrying once more the tricolour from capital to
capital . . . in a way which would not arouse the hostility of
nations but . . . set them free',[2] the Germans replied with the
Wacht am Rhein; similarly in 1848, none, except the extremest
Republicans, would have brooked French intrusion, and these
only by an ultra-revolutionary France which would have given
victory to their cause. The February Revolution quickened the
movement towards German unity, both by parallel and by
contrary impulses—national sovereignty, overriding dynastic
rights, was a precondition of German unity if this was to be
achieved without war, while the desire to safeguard social order
and the national territory made Germans draw together: both
these motives were almost invariably present in greater or less
degree.

But there was fear of intervention and war from yet another
quarter: in progressive circles fear of Russia overshadowed that
of France. On 13 March the Rhenish Liberal, Camphausen
(who on the 28th became Prussian Premier), wrote to the
Minister of the Interior, von Bodelschwingh, about the danger
of a separatist movement rising in southern and western Germany under French influence unless Prussia took the lead in
a national constitutional movement: 'Germany will be rent in

[1] Op. cit., vol. i, pp. 102–3.
[2] In an article in *Le Temps* quoted by Thureau-Dangin, *Histoire de la
Monarchie de Juillet*, vol. iv, p. 234.

two. And where would the frontier run between South and North Germany? The will of Governments cannot decide, for Germans do not shoot at Germans, but all will take up arms against the Russians'[1]—an abrupt and seemingly irrelevant *finale*. When on 21 March Frederick William IV proclaimed that 'Prussia henceforth merges into Germany',·and that for the 'days of danger' he assumed the leadership, he first spoke of 'supreme danger', next of 'extraneous danger from more than one direction', and in the third sentence of 'this imminent double danger'.[2] A week later, in a memorandum for his Ministers, in which he tried to attenuate the ultra-German emphasis of the proclamation, he described the German people, 'of over 40 millions', as predestined to form 'the bulwark of Europe against revolution and despotism, both of which everywhere endanger social order and all true legal freedom'.[3] His naming of Russia as a danger was lip-service to the *Zeitgeist*: when the National Assembly met at Frankfort, numerous motions and petitions demanded an alliance with France, a transfer of troops from the western to the eastern frontier of Germany, 'prompt arming against Russia', &c. The Committee for Foreign Affairs, reporting on them on 1 July, declared against ideological war of any kind; between Germany and France there should be no hostility or struggle (only a 'noble rivalry' in freedom, its right application, and in 'true respect for the rule of law'); but a long, hesitant, and yet basically inimical paragraph was devoted to Russia: the apprehended danger of attack has been carefully considered; Russian troop-concentrations are not necessarily directed against Germany, and their size has been greatly exaggerated; still, it is a fact that Russian troops on the German frontier have been reinforced; but the necessary counter-measures cannot be determined by the Assembly. The report concluded with the following resolution, which was carried: 'That the German forces on the eastern frontier should be rendered sufficiently strong to be fully able to stand up to the army which faces them.'[4]

[1] See *König Friedrich Wilhelms IV Briefwechsel mit Ludolf Camphausen*, edited by Erich Brandenburg (1906), Appendix, p. 219.

[2] See A. Wolff, *Berliner Revolutions-Chronik* (1851), vol. i, pp. 298–9.

[3] Brandenburg, *Briefwechsel*, p. 21.

[4] See *Stenographischer Bericht über die Verhandlungen der deutschen constituierenden Nationalversammlung zu Frankfurt am Main*, vol. i, pp. 654–5. Here are the most important passages about ideological war: 'Germany . . . will never put her hand to a struggle of various States for political principles', as she wishes to preserve 'the movement . . . which has gripped a whole Continent, and is

Hatred of Tsarist Russia, as the mainstay of the Holy Alliance and the guardian of autocracy, was universal among European Liberals and Radicals. Russian intervention on the side of the monarchs was feared in progressive, and hoped for in reactionary, German circles: the Government in St. Petersburg, presided over by a dynasty which in every generation intermarried with German princely families, and was served at home and abroad by multitudes of Germans, Baltic and immigrant, was very nearly a German 'colonial' outpost, isolated from liberalizing influences, but deriving from its vast Slav Empire a force with which it threatened to dominate Germany—a super-Prussia beyond Germany's borders. Leopold von Gerlach, a leading member of the Prussian Court *camarilla*, said to the Russian Ambassador, Baron von Meyendorff, that in Germany 'order could not be restored without the help of foreign Powers'. 'I told him how happy I was that he, a German, was here Ambassador, because the best Russian could not have understood our conditions (*Verhältnisse*).'[1] When reading the correspondence of Count Nesselrode with Baron von Meyendorff, or the letters which Nicholas I wrote to his brother-in-law Frederick William IV, one feels that here were outlandish Germans[2] using the French language and representing a Power which stood for a principle of authority rather than for a national cause: as such more easily consulted and called in, and more ready to play the mentor.[3]

well-nigh without precedent in history, from degenerating into a universal war between the nations, and from destroying the finest of its own achievements'.

[1] *Denkwürdigkeiten aus dem Leben Leopold von Gerlachs* (1891), vol. i, p. 197.

[2] Bismarck mentions in a dispatch from St. Petersburg, on 26 May 1859, that the discussion in Council, held in the presence of the Emperor before Nesselrode's departure, was in French, because 'Count Nesselrode and Herr von Meyendorff do not express themselves with ease in the Russian language'; see L. Raschdau, *Die politischen Berichte des Fürsten Bismarck aus Petersburg und Paris* (1920), vol. i, p. 84. Circourt writes about Meyendorff: 'He is a German nobleman with the rectitude and *Gemüth* which do honour to his race: at the same time a loyal, devoted but discerning servant of the Russian Government and Imperial House . . .' (*Souvenirs*, vol. i, pp. 130–1); and about Count Medem, Russian Ambassador in Vienna: 'a true gentleman, German in character and manners' (ibid., p. 340).

[3] Thus on 28 Feb. 1848, Meyendorff reports to Nesselrode having talked very freely to the Prussian Premier, Count Canitz, about the line which Prussia should adopt towards the French Revolution—'ces gens-ci ne doivent pas faire à eux seuls de la grande politique, parcequ'ils n'y entendent rien'. See *Briefwechsel*, vol. ii, p. 37.

In Germany the conviction was general in the first months of the revolution that a great inner transformation could not be achieved without war against Russia which had a double interest in the maintenance of the *status quo*: a union of Germany as a sovereign nation would have run counter both to the power-politics and to the autocratic principles of the Russian Empire—nor is it easy to determine where the one interest began or the other ended.[1]

X

For war against Russia, Poland was the obvious spearhead, and anti-Russian feeling was apt to mix, as it so often does, with pro-Polish enthusiasms. The collapse of the Polish revolution in 1831 was followed by mass-emigration—of members of the Government and of the Diet, of the aristocracy and the landed gentry, of the intelligentsia (in the most brilliant period of Polish literature), and of large bodies of the defeated, disbanding army. Seldom if ever has there been such an exodus of a nation's *élite*, and for the next fifteen years the centre of Polish intellectual life and political activities shifted abroad, mainly to France. These *émigrés* did not forsake their country but carried it with them. They did not leave in opposition to any part of their own people, but as its true spokesmen. Indeed, at times, the idea was seriously canvassed of reconvening the Polish Diet in Paris on the strength of a resolution passed at its last sitting in Warsaw, on 18 September 1831, that it should follow the army and be free to meet anywhere, with thirty-three members for quorum.[2]

---

[1] The question of Russia's attitude towards German union is most fully dealt with in J. Feldman, op. cit. A few years earlier it was posed by Erich Marcks in a lecture 'Die europäischen Mächte und die 48-er Revolution', published in the *Historische Zeitschrift*, vol. cxlii (1930).

[2] According to Gadon, *Emigracya polska* (1902), vol. ii, p. 205, in Jan. 1833 50 members of the late Diet were abroad, 34 of them in Paris. According to Lewak (chapter on the 'Great Emigration' in S. Lam, *Polska, jej dzieje i kultura* (1937), vol. iii, p. 207) in that month 25 members declared for, and 12 against reconstituting the Polish Diet in Paris. The idea (which had the enthusiastic support of Mickiewicz) was finally dropped, the Reds opposing it because they considered the late Diet unrepresentative and blamed it for the defeat, and the Whites, because they feared to provoke the Partitioning Powers and force France to take action. The idea of the 'Diet in Exile' was revived in 1846, and was pressed in 1848, when Austrian and Prussian Poland obtained parliamentary representation, but not Russian Poland. On 16 May, 14 members met in Paris and summoned a wider assembly, but apparently were no longer able to convene a quorum; see *Korespondencya J. B. Zaleskiego*, edited by D. Zaleski (1900), vol. ii, pp. 47 and 97–100.

When in that autumn nearly 50,000 Polish soldiers crossed into Prussia and Austria, some of the leaders planned to take them to France, as 'ready cadres for future Polish Legions which, in a universal European upheaval, would sally forth to conquer Poland's independence'.[1] But an amnesty for the non-commissioned ranks,[2] published by the Tsar on 1 November 1831, and seconded by the zealous endeavours of the two Germanic Powers, made a great many soldiers recross the frontier, and in the end only a few thousand, mostly officers, started the trek for the west. The total of the 'emigration' is estimated at almost 10,000,[3] about three-fourths belonging to the educated classes.

The path of the refugees led across Germany, and, though frowned upon by the Austrian and Prussian Governments, they were fêted by the population as fighters for freedom and victims of Tsarism—this was the time of the *Polenlieder*[4] and the *Polenschwärmerei*. But it was in France that these men hoped to reform their ranks, and from France to restart the struggle— they remembered the Polish legions of the Great Revolution and Napoleon,[5] and the French armies marching across Europe

[1] See J. Frejlich, 'Legion Jenerała Józefa Bema w walce o sukcesję portugalską' ('The Legion of Gen. J. Bem in the War of Portuguese Succession') in the *Przegląd Historyczny* (*Historical Review*), vol. xiv (1912).

[2] This limitation was subsequently removed thanks to British intercession: but the amnesty was not honestly adhered to for either category.

[3] Krasnowski, in his *Almanach historique, ou Souvenir de l'Émigration polonaise* (1846) supplies a list of about 8,500 names; but such lists are bound to be incomplete, and Gadon (op. cit., vol. iii, p. 232) puts the total number at 9,500–10,000. Both estimates are of the total that left Poland, not of the number abroad at any one time. Lewak (op. cit., vol. iii, p. 199) attempts a census for 1839, and arrives at the following figures:

In France	5,758
Algiers, the Foreign Legion, and the French Colonies	500
Great Britain, at least	1,300
Belgium	300
Spain	500
America	500
Switzerland, Germany, Scandinavia, Italy	300
Together about	9,000

Of the *émigrés* in France, 5,260 were in receipt of Government subsidies, and in Great Britain 600.

[4] In the 1830's, Moser's 'Die letzten Zehn vom vierten Regiment' was one of the most popular songs in Germany.

[5] Although in reality Napoleon, all along, fought shy of the Poles, the Napoleonic legend was cherished by them, even more than by the French. Perhaps the finest poem on the return of Napoleon's body to France was written by Słowacki. Mickiewicz remained a votary of the 'Napoleonic

till they reached the Vistula and the Niemen: and they saw the Tricolour unfurled once more. They forgot their disappointments of twenty and thirty years ago,[1] and failed to gauge the spirit of 1830. A Polish lady wrote from Paris, in December 1831: 'The King, the Government, and the upper classes do not like us, but in the French manner *ils enveloppent leurs sentiments de belles phrases. . . .* We are truly beloved by the second rank of society and by the common people, and we therefore arouse fear.'[2] To the Legitimists the Tsar was the high priest of their creed; the July Monarchy was intent on establishing its respectability *vis-à-vis* Europe, and on avoiding further revolutionary complications; while the Left did the Poles harm by passionately espousing their cause, by encouraging them in the belief that a universal European upheaval was near, and by using them, sojourners in a strange land and pensioners of a foreign government, as a stick with which to beat that Government. Lafayette proclaimed: ' Toute la France est polonaise '; and Louis Blanc wrote in retrospect: 'Nous vivions surtout en Pologne.' Henceforth every year an embarrassing resolution and debate on Poland was repeated in the French Parliament— a meaningless gesture repeated *ad nauseam*.[3]

The July Monarchy, even if they enveloped their sentiments in fine phrases, at least did not hide hard facts from the Poles, nor their own basic attitude. But when in January 1831 some Polish emissaries waylaid in Prussia the Duc de Mortemart,

idea' even under Napoleon III, and by his Bonapartism disconcerted and estranged many of his collaborators in the *Tribune des Peuples*; for Herzen's account of the inaugural dinner on 24 Feb. 1849, when Mickiewicz was to have given the toast of the Revolution of 1848, but finished by invoking the shade of Napoleon, see *Byloye i dumy (Reminiscences), Polnoye Sobranye (Collected Works)*, part iv, vol. 13, pp. 310–11 (1919). The Napoleonic tradition was revived in Poland shortly before 1914, and had a considerable influence on the development of the Piłsudski movement and legend.

[1] Guizot writes in his *Mémoires*, vol. ii, p. 274: '. . . ni la Révolution française, ni l'Empereur Napoléon n'ont fait entrer le rétablissement de la Pologne dans leurs réels et énergiques desseins. On a prononcé des paroles; on a entr'ouvert des perspectives; on a exploité des dévouements en provoquant des espérances; rien de plus. L'extrême malheur a pu seul puiser quelques illusions dans de tels mensonges. Tout le monde s'est servi de la Pologne; personne ne l'a jamais servie.'

[2] See Gadon, op. cit., vol. ii, p. 8.

[3] Lamartine writes in his *Histoire de la Révolution de 1848* (vol. ii, p. 156): 'For the past eighteen years, the French Parliament, constrained rather than convinced, at the opening of each session pronounced a sterile wish on behalf of Poland. The wishes of a great nation are derision if they are but an empty sound, unsupported by action.'

then on a mission to St. Petersburg, and he told them the truth
about their situation, they would have none of it: 'French
democracy will determine events; and French democracy will
support Poland. Your King and your Cabinet will be forced
by public opinion to come to our help. . . . The issue is joined,
and it will be all or nothing.' Mortemart replied: '*Eh bien*, I
grieve to have to say it, but I am deeply convinced: it will
be nothing.'[1] And Casimir Périer said in Parliament, on
21 February 1832, in answering the Opposition: 'No, gentlemen, the misfortunes of the Poles should not be laid at the door
of the French Government, but of those who gave them bad
advice.'[2] The Poles drew their own conclusions. Mochnacki
wrote in August 1831: '. . . not the Cabinets are our allies, but
the peoples.'[3] And General Umiński in 1833: '. . . all our hope
is in nations rising in revolution.'[4] And Mickiewicz: 'There can
be no alliance between Poland and the Governments. . . . The
enemies of the old order in Europe are our only allies.'[5]

No wonder then if the French Government, harried by
Republican conspiracies and Russian remonstrances, tried to
keep the Poles away from Paris. The soldiers were sent to
dépôts, first at Avignon, Besançon, and Bourges, but after some
revolutionary escapades, they were dispersed between some 180
small places, at a distance from the German, Swiss, and Pied-
montese frontiers: they were kept in honourable semi-confine-
ment, on meagre allowances, with no duties to perform,
regimented yet undisciplined and idle. Little was left to them
but to ponder over the past, dream about the future, spin
schemes however fantastic, and quarrel among themselves.
Even in Paris life was miserable. The poet Bohdan Zaleski
wrote on 4 December 1833: 'With hearts unbearably void, we
are sad and bored. To-day the same as yesterday, to-morrow
as to-day: from morning to night in a dense fog which never
lifts. . . .'[6] And Konarski, on 25 September 1834: 'I sit indoors,
muse, dream, sometimes play the flute, and sigh for home . . .
I eat, sleep, and work like an ox, but the human side of life

---

[1] See Victor de Nouvion, *Histoire du règne de Louis-Philippe*, vol. ii, p. 191.
Guizot mentions (*Mémoires*, ii, p. 280) having been assured by Mortemart
that the account as given by Nouvion was accurate.

[2] Quoted after Thureau-Dangin, op. cit., vol. i, ch. v, p. 487.

[3] See A. Sliwiński, *Mickiewicz jako polityk* (*Mickiewicz as a Politician*) (1908),
p. 74.

[4] Ibid., p. 78.

[5] Ibid., p. 74.

[6] D. Zaleski, op. cit., vol. i, p. 53.

has been taken from us.'[1] And Wielogłowski in his memoirs: 'God and our people will have mercy upon us, and forgive us our shortcomings, because of our great sufferings and our longing for home, which very nearly drove us mad.'[2]

Like all *émigrés* they had thought that the separation would be short, and now years went by, while they were searching in a hopeless, fumbling manner for some way of serving the cause. Only a handful went into the Foreign Legion, which the French Government had suggested to suit its own convenience. But even Prince Adam Czartoryski, a statesman of European reputation and experience, favoured in 1832–3 the scheme of a Polish Legion to fight in Portugal for Donna Maria da Gloria against Don Miguel, as representing the system of the Holy Alliance: the Poles should do so 'in their own interest', for the cause of all nations is one, and (a much more cogent reason) because it would rescue them from the idleness which undermines 'their capacities, minds, and morals'.[3] About the same time the Turkish Ambassador in Vienna proposed to Czartoryski a transfer of the entire Polish emigration to Turkey, there to reorganize the army and administration. But when the Turks secured Russia's help against Egypt, they dropped the Poles, who now turned to Mehmet Ali. General Dembiński proceeded to Cairo.[4] So went on the weary round of bizarre negotiations in exotic quarters, from which 'only extreme misfortune could draw some illusory hopes'.[5] Still, the great mass of the Polish emigration was opposed to frittering away forces, and awaited the time for direct action in the very heart of Europe. They developed a creed, by no means free of exaltation and of illusions, yet based on premisses which were sound though postulating things not easy of realization. They saw that Poland's resurrection could only come through a war between the Partitioning Powers, or the defeat of all three (as happened in 1918); that this presupposed a general upheaval, a world

---

[1] M. Handelsman, *Rozwój narodowości nowoczesnej* (*The Development of Modern Nationality*), chapter on 'The Emigration and Europe' (1926), p. 130.

[2] Gadon, op. cit., vol. iii, p. 262.

[3] See Frejlich, op. cit.

[4] See A. Lewak, *Dzieje emigracji polskiej w Turcji, 1831–1878* (*The History of the Polish Emigration in Turkey*) (1935).

[5] These schemes and their authors—high-minded, unbalanced, interested, or just trying to get rid of the Polish *émigrés*—vividly remind one of recent schemes for settling Jews in any Arctic or tropical Timbuktu, so that they should not be a nuisance in Western countries, nor press for a return to their own National Home.

war or a world revolution; that the July Monarchy, which was steadily moving to the Right, offered no base against the Powers of the Holy Alliance; and that a new revolution was needed, to mobilize popular forces in France and give the signal to Europe. They waited for 1848.

XI

Mickiewicz wrote: 'Poland will re-arise and free all nations of Europe from bondage. *Ibi patria, ubi male*; wherever in Europe liberty is suppressed and is fought for, there is the battle of your country.'[1] And he prayed: 'For the universal war for the freedom of nations, we beseech thee, O Lord!'[2]

But Lamartine, spokesman of the Second Republic in its early days, took a different view of the Polish cause and the French, and European, interest. 'France, no doubt, owed much to that brave and unhappy nation, but not the sacrifice of her policy and of world peace.'[3] 'Tout leur est patrie pourvu qu'ils l'agitent.'[4]

The Poles are the ferment of Europe. Bold in battle and turbulent in the public arena, they are the revolutionary army of the Continent. They tried to raise Paris and threatened the Government. . . . For their sake to declare war on Prussia, Austria, and Russia, would have meant a crusade for the conquest of a sepulchre. Refuse it to them? This meant to expose oneself to unpopularity and revolts. . . . Lamartine, who watched carefully their proceedings, felt indignant at having more trouble in restraining these guests of France than in restraining France herself.[5]

In replying to a Polish deputation, he exclaimed: 'We love Poland, we love Italy, we love all the oppressed nations, but most of all we love France, and we bear the responsibility for her fate, and perhaps for that of Europe at this moment.'[6] And in the parliamentary debate on Poland, on 23 May 1848, he argued that France must not try to act alone—the suggestion of 'a second campaign against Moscow . . . across a Germany violated in her territory, dignity, . . . in her national feelings', could only originate with people who have 'never looked at a map nor measured the distance from the Vistula to the Rhine'.[7]

---

[1] *Księgi narodu polskiego i pielgrzymstwa polskiego* (*The Books of the Polish Nation and of the Polish Pilgrims*) (1832), p. 81.   [2] Ibid., p. 93.
[3] *Histoire de la Révolution de 1848* (1849), vol. ii, p. 156.   [4] Ibid., p. 256.
[5] Ibid., pp. 256–7.   [6] *Trois mois au pouvoir* (1848), p. 133.
[7] Cf. Sebastiani's speech in Parliament on 28 Jan. 1831: 'Que pouvons nous faire pour la Pologne? Ce sont les campagnes de Napoléon qu'on nous propose.'

Joint action by the Great Powers was required—'by France, England, and most of all, by a Germany interested as much as ourselves in the restoration of that great bulwark of Western civilization'. A year later he wrote: 'France could not reach Poland except through the intermediary of Germany, and in a general replanning (*remaniement*) of the Continent.'[1]

By the Germans Poland was looked upon as 'a bulwark of civilization' so long as they considered war with Russia desirable or unavoidable; and not by Austrian Germans alone, who were already conscious of the inevitable clash between the Habsburg Monarchy and Russia,[2] but by Germans from the Rhine and Main,[3] and even by Prussians. The forerunner of Pan-Germanism, Ernst Moritz Arndt, who in 1811–13 had found refuge in Russia, descanted in 1843, in his *Essay on Comparative History*, upon the danger of Russia advancing into Europe, and the need of re-creating Poland as an 'intermediary State' (*ein Mittelreich*) between East and West.[4] In March 1848 the leading Liberal papers in Germany demanded war against Russia. On 25 March the *Kölnische Zeitung* wrote about 'emancipation' from St. Petersburg, and 'the flaming hatred of Russia' which filled the hearts of the Germans; and on the 26th the *Augsburger Allgemeine Zeitung* described the past Prussian policy of subservience to Russia as the main cause of the revolution. The historian Gervinus, who edited the Heidelberg *Allgemeine Deutsche Zeitung*, declared the restoration of Poland a matter of justice, and still more of political common sense, and claimed territory for her stretching from the Baltic to the Black Sea. Similar demands appeared in other papers: the Russians were to be thrown back beyond the Dvina and the Dnieper, and a powerful Poland was to be established between those

---

[1] *Histoire de la Révolution de 1848*, vol. ii, p. 156.

[2] See, for instance, Schuselka's book on *Deutschland, Polen und Russland* (1846) or Anton Springer's essay in the *Jahrbücher der Gegenwart*, for Apr. 1848; also E. Müsebeck, *Anton Springer als nationaler Politiker des deutschen Liberalismus* (1932).

[3] See, for instance, diary of a certain Dr. L. Ladenburg, a banker at Mannheim, under date of 25 Mar. 1848, in L. Mathy, *Aus dem Nachlass von Karl Mathy*, 1898 (p. 150): 'The restoration of Poland and the humiliation of Russia is desired by all Germans'—but 'shall we be able at the same time to build up our constitution (*uns konstituieren*) and wage war on Russia?'

[4] *Versuch in vergleichender Völkergeschichte*, p. 323. He wrote about the Russians: '... the entire nation hates us Germans, and despises us' (p. 315); and further: '. . . thank God, that differences of outlook have opened so wide a chasm between the Russians and the Poles' (p. 325).

'barbarians' and Germany, 'more valuable to her than two discontented provinces'.[1]

Here the *Realpolitik* of the German Liberals, which masqueraded as high idealism, committed its first miscalculation: it assumed that a Polish State in its pre-1772 frontiers was viable, and would be powerful. If in 1848 the national character of a country could still have been determined by the language and politics of the landowning class and the intelligentsia, these vast territories would have been Polish; but in treating them as such, the imaginative forgers (in both senses) of the world's destinies took no account of the peasants' hatred of the landlords, which even in the seventeenth century set the Ukraine ablaze and in 1812 produced peasant revolts in White Russia, or of the rising nationalisms which in 1848 made the Ruthenes in East Galicia turn violently against the Poles, and the subject nationalities of Hungary go to war against the Magyars. Such regard for social superiorities and disregard of the rights of the masses is comprehensible in middle-class intellectuals, but is comic when displayed by men who professed Socialist principles and preached class war: in reality they differed but little from their milieu—tendencies, venom, or colouring vary, but the basic misapprehensions and nonsense of contemporaries are remarkably alike. When on 15 May the Paris mob invaded the Chamber of Deputies shouting *Vive la Pologne!* Blanqui, a revolutionary who under five *régimes* spent some thirty-five years (almost half his life) in prison, summoned the Assembly 'to decree that France will not sheathe the sword till Poland is integrally reconstituted in her old frontiers of 1772'.[2] He said:

... let not the National Assembly fear the ill-humour of Europe; ... if its will is firmly expressed and is sustained by a French army on the Rhine, any obstacles which diplomacy might raise will collapse of themselves, so that ancient Poland, the Poland of 1772 [the people here recalled the date], the Poland of 1772 [bravos and applause from the people] should re-arise within her frontiers.

And Armand Barbès, another perennial prison plant, having for an hour established his 'Government' at the Hôtel-de-Ville, issued the following proclamation:[3]

The Provisional Government, attentive to the wishes of the people, declares that it will immediately give to the Russian and German

[1] The above quotations from the German press are reproduced from Feldman, op. cit.
[2] According to the *Moniteur*, as quoted by Garnier-Pagès, *Histoire de la Révolution de 1848* (1869), vol. ix, pp. 186–7.   [3] Ibid., pp. 254–5.

Governments an order to restore Poland, and that, should these Governments fail to obey the order, the Government of the Republic will immediately declare war on them.

The frontiers were not named, but he, too, thought of nothing less than those of 1772.

So did Marx and Engels who, on 19 August 1848, wrote in the *Neue Rheinische Zeitung*:[1]

The establishment of a democratic Poland is a primary condition for the establishment of a democratic Germany . . . not of a sham Poland, but of a viable State. She must receive at least the frontiers of 1772, and . . . a considerable stretch of coast at least on the Baltic. . . .

—the second 'at least' implying as admissible another stretch on the Black Sea! Four years later, even the stretch on the Baltic was to be at the expense of Russia: 'The Poles', wrote Engels in February 1852, 'by receiving extended territories in the east, would have become more tractable and reasonable in the west; and Riga and Mitau would have been deemed, after all, quite as important to them as Danzig and Elbing.'[2]

Were Marx and Engels under any misapprehension concerning the national character of those 'extended territories in the east'? 'If people say that to demand the restoration of Poland is to appeal to the principle of nationality', wrote Engels in *The Commonwealth*[3] in 1866, '. . . they do not know what they are talking about, for the restoration of Poland means the re-establishment of a State composed of at least four different nationalities' (Poles, Lithuanians, White and Little Russians). He draws a distinction between the 'principle of nationalities', inscribed by Napoleon III on his banner, and 'the right of the great European *nations* to separate and independent national existence', and contemptuously brushes aside any claims to such an existence on the part of 'those numerous small relics of peoples which, after having figured for a longer or shorter period on the stage of history, were finally absorbed as integral portions into one or the other of those more powerful nations . . . .'. 'The principle of nationalities' is 'nothing but a Russian invention concocted to destroy Poland',[4] just as Pan-Slavism is

---

[1] See F. Mehring, *Gesammelte Schriften von Karl Marx und Friedrich Engels 1841–50*, vol. iii (1902), pp. 149–50.

[2] See in *Revolution and Counter-Revolution, or Germany in 1848*, chapter on 'Poles, Czechs, and Germans'.

[3] Reprinted in an Appendix to N. Rjasanoff's essay on 'Karl Marx und Friedrich Engels über die Polenfrage', in the *Archiv für die Geschichte des Sozialismus und der Arbeiterbewegung*, vol. vi (1916).

[4] Engels even reproaches Russia with having adhered to that principle:

its application by Russia 'to the Serbians, Croats, Ruthenes, Czechs, and other remnants of by-gone Slavonian peoples in Turkey, Hungary, and Germany'. In short, Engels seems to have realized the community of interest which existed with regard to the 'subject races' between the Germans, Magyars, Poles, and even the Turks, and either to have overlooked, or deliberately ignored, the fact that the dominion of those *Herrenvölker* was based on social superiority. The idea that the new Poland was to be 'democratic' and arise through a peasant revolution within frontiers drawn on the basis of Polish *latifundia*, points to a high degree of mental incoherence: for the one thing which that Greater Poland could not have survived would have been a Russian peasant revolution.[1] Nor was there any deep love of the Poles, or appreciation of them, which moved that hearty, honest Teuton, Engels. In between his pro-Polish effusions of 1848 and of 1866, he wrote to Marx from Manchester on 23 May 1851:[2]

The more I think about this business, the clearer it is to me that the Poles are *une nation foutue*, a serviceable instrument only till Russia herself is swept into the agrarian revolution. From that moment Poland loses all *raison d'être*. The Poles have never done anything in history except engage in brave, blatant foolery (*tapfere, krakeelsüchtige Dummheit gespielt*). . . . 'Immortal' about the Poles is only their baseless

'The first and foremost ambition of Russia is the union of all Russian tribes under the Tsar . . . and among these she includes White and Little Russia. And in order to prove that her ambition went no further, she took very good care, during the three partitions, to annex none but White and Little Russian provinces, leaving the country inhabited by Poles, and even a portion of Little Russia (Eastern Galicia) to her accomplices' (*Archiv für die Geschichte des Sozialismus und der Arbeiterbewegung*, vol. vi (1916), p. 217).

[1] The Poles themselves were conscious of it, especially since 1846. In 1863 the Russian revolutionary Bakunin went to Stockholm, planning to go to Russia with a view to raising a peasant revolution in support of the Polish national rising. On 1 Aug. he wrote to Herzen and Ogarev, after a talk with one of the Polish revolutionaries: 'Do you know what Demontowicz finally said to me? That so far from desiring a Russian revolution, he fears it as a dreadful evil, and that if he had to choose between a new victory of Tsarism and Poland being saved through a Russian revolution, he would prefer Tsarism to be victorious for the time being, because sooner or later it will be possible to shake off Tsarism, while a Russian social revolution, by opening the sluices of Polish barbarism, would irrevocably drown Polish civilisation' (see *Pisma M. A. Bakunina k A. I. Herzenu i N. P. Ogarevu*, edited by M. P. Dragomanov (1896), pp. 124–5).

[2] See *Karl Marx, Friedrich Engels, Briefwechsel*, edited by D. Rjazanov (1929), part iii, vol. i, pp. 206–7; the letter is included in the English selection, *K. Marx and F. Engels, Correspondence, 1846–1895* (1934).

hullabaloo. . . . One-fourth of Poland speaks Lithuanian, one-fourth Ruthene, a small part semi-Russian, and of Poland proper fully a third is Germanised.

Fortunately in the *Neue Rheinische Zeitung* we have assumed no commitments towards Poland except the unavoidable concerning restoration with a suitable frontier—and even this on condition that there is an agrarian revolution. I am sure that this revolution will materialize in Russia before it does in Poland. . . .

Conclusion: Take away from the Poles in the West as much as possible; under pretext of defence, garrison their fortresses with Germans, let them make a mess of things for themselves, send them into the fire, eat up their land, palm them off with mirages of Riga and Odessa, and if the Russians can be got to move, form an alliance with them, and force the Poles to give in. Every inch ceded between Memel and Cracow completely ruins an anyhow miserably weak frontier. . . .

Besides, I am convinced that in the next brawl, the whole Polish insurrection will be limited to the Posnanian and Galician gentry, with a few stragglers from Russian Poland. . . . A nation which can at best muster 20,000–30,000 men, has no voice. . . .

In short, the difference between the apostles of German Social Democracy, the exponents of German Liberalism in the Frankfort Parliament, and the Prussian *Junkers*, concerned merely the point in time when they reached the acme of *Realpolitik*, the degree of sincerity with which they admitted it in public, and the means they had of translating their views into practice.

XII

If any one family could be named as representative of the 'Third Germany' (of the smaller States in contradistinction to Austria and Prussia), and of the nationalism of the German Liberals in 1848, it is that of the old *Reichsfreiherr* Hans von Gagern, which until 1801 had been *reichsunmittelbar* (i.e. had owed allegiance only to the Empire). Of his sons, the eldest, Friedrich, was a General in the Dutch service, but in 1848 returned to Germany, and was killed on 20 April, fighting the Republicans in Baden; the third, Heinrich, became in March 1848 Prime Minister of Hesse-Darmstadt, was from May to December 1848 President of the German National Assembly, and from December 1848 till May 1849 Prime Minister of the shadow-Germany at Frankfort; and the youngest, Max, was in the Nassau diplomatic service, and a member of the Frankfort Assembly. The three brothers were among the foremost exponents of a German Empire under the King of Prussia, but German, and not 'specifically Prussian', in character. Their correspondence, papers, and writings illustrate the German attitude towards Russia and the Poles in the early stages of the revolution.[1]

'War, and perhaps war on two fronts, seems to me unavoidable', wrote Friedrich to Heinrich from The Hague, on 1 April 1848. And further: 'War between Germany and Russia is considered probable . . . *our* inclinations are for it.'[2] Early in March 1848 Max von Gagern persuaded the Duke of Nassau to send him on a mission to other German Princes in order to persuade them to take the lead in the German national movement, and thus give it a monarchical character.[3] He was successful in Hesse-Darmstadt, Baden, Württemberg, less so in Bavaria; but when, on 21 March, he arrived in Berlin, via Dresden, he found the town *en pleine révolution*. On 21 and 22 March he saw the new Prussian Minister for Foreign Affairs, Baron Heinrich von Arnim, expounded to him the scheme of German Union under Prussia after she had merged into Germany (she was to have no Diet of her own, but dissolve into her eight provinces, each about the size of a middle-sized German State), and then said: 'What your King has promised the Poles, implies war against Russia.' 'Gagern', writes his biographer, 'advised to start that war, for the highly excited nation should be supplied with an object for its hostility: thus alone would unification be possible.'[4] On 22 March Max von Gagern, on his way back to Dresden, scribbled in the train a note to Heinrich: '. . . I see only one means of salvation: we must force the King of Prussia, now German King, to liberate, to restore Poland, perhaps be her elected King. Therefore war with Russia. In any case, I return to Berlin, and shall show the King himself where his last chance lies. . . .' The next day, Gagern, accompanied by Count Lehrbach and Herr von Sternenfels, representing Hesse-Darm-

---

[1] See especially Heinrich von Gagern, *Das Leben des Generals Friedrich von Gagern* (1857), and L. von Pastor, *Leben des Freiherrn Max von Gagern, 1810–1889* (1912).

[2] See H. von Gagern, op. cit., pp. 669–70. In the early days of the revolution, there were even Conservatives who, for different reasons, favoured war with Russia. Thus, e.g., Major von Randow wrote from Berlin to General von Colomb, G.C.O. Poznań, on 31 Mar.: 'Many people think that war with Russia is the only means of saving the Fatherland, by throwing the scum against the bullets of the enemy' ('damit man die Hefe gegen die feindlichen Kugeln werfe'); see Otto Hoetzsch, 'Die Stellung des Generals von Colomb zur Revolution in Posen und zu Willisen', in the *Zeitschrift für Osteuropäische Geschichte*, vol. iv (1914), p. 364.

[3] Pastor, op. cit., pp. 182–5.   [4] Ibid., p. 230.

stadt and Württemberg, was received by the King in the presence
of Arnim. After Gagern had spoken about the position in
Germany, the King, moved to tears, asked his advice, for, he
said, 'I recognise that Germany is in full dissolution'—so
Gagern reported to his Duke on 23 March; and he continued:[1]

Thereupon I said these words, attested by Count Lehrbach and Herr
von Sternenfels: 'Your Majesty will permit me in this solemn hour to
touch upon matters completely outside my official instructions. What
your Majesty has done and announced in the last few days to save
Germany from imminent danger would, *before* March 18, have united
us all and secured us . . . against any movement, from outside or inside
. . . now only a new, and still bolder, decision—to wage foreign war—
can save us from anarchy and dissolution. But not as your Majesty
has hinted, a war against France, which at present would not be
acceptable, but a war against Russia.'
The King: 'What? Aggression against Russia?'
Me: 'Freeing the Poles will entail war with Russia.'
The King: 'But Poland will never re-arise. She is at peace and the
strongest measures have been taken.'
Me: 'Seeing the magic influence which the idea of nationality now
exercises, how can we hope to strengthen the unity of our own nation,
and to assert our own nationality, if we oppress and flout that of others?
Only a liberation of Poland can save your Majesty and us all.'
The King: 'By God, never, never shall I draw the sword against
Russia.'
Me: 'Then I look upon Germany as lost.'

Max von Gagern, who was a convert to Rome, may have felt
more strongly about Poland than the average German. But he
wrote this report for his prince, a Protestant; and the analysis
of the situation, published by Heinrich in 1857,[2] though cleverly
retouched on one vital point, reproduces the atmosphere and
arguments of those days. In the light of subsequent events,
Heinrich von Gagern retrospectively reserves in the first sentence
Germany's claim to any late Polish territories which had been
(or were alleged to have been) 'successfully Germanised' (and
the sentence is so exceptionally tortuous that no other language
but German can do justice to its peculiar quality):

There must have been few among those taking an active part in the
German movement who would not have considered it a matter of
justice, indeed of political wisdom, to restore Poland within such
frontiers as were drawn by the numerical superiority already achieved
by a population of German nationality on soil which had previously

[1] Ibid., p. 234.   [2] Op. cit., vol. ii, pp. 775–6.

been Polish.[1] . . . To the great and permanent interest which Germany has in the restoration of an independent Poland, another was added of a specific and temporary nature. Sooner or later, war with Russia had to come, over the Baltic Sea and the Baltic Provinces, over Poland, over the Danube and the Eastern Question, lastly over Slesvig-Holstein; and it seemed advisable to hasten it. A new united Germany had 'to enter history not with freedoms only, but with deeds'. War against Russia would have been the most popular war throughout Germany; it offered the most wholesome remedy for reducing the existing ferment, and the most effective for countering the dislike of a standing army which thirty years of peace had fostered in the nation. . . .

In short, the Gagern family favoured war against Russia, and among their reasons were some not dissimilar to those which inspired, and were proved valid by, that against France in 1870: the war was considered unavoidable, it would have healed internal divisions and furthered the work of unification, and it would have rendered the army popular in Germany. Forerunners of the modern Pan-German Imperialists, the Gagerns envisaged as inevitable a conflict with Russia over the problem of 1914 ('the Danube and the Eastern Question') and over territory claimed in 1918 (the Baltic Provinces), neither of which Bismarck, in his self-restraint of a true statesman,[2] would ever agree, even at the height of his power, to include in the ambit of German interests and aims. And naturally men who thought of the Baltic Provinces as German, because of the language spoken by a thin stratum of their landowning class and intelligentsia, could also contemplate the possibility of a Poland within the frontiers of the old 'Gentry Republic'. On the other hand, the gravity of the inevitable conflict between the Poles and the Germans in 'previously Polish' territories, did not dawn as yet on the leaders of the German national movement in the south and west, or even in Berlin: and this was the second miscalculation of Liberal *Realpolitik* in March 1848. Posnania and the Polish question, as well as Bohemia, were, in the short span of a few months, to show up German 'National Liberalism'. During the subsequent years of reaction, these facts were over-

---

[1] Here is the sentence in the original: 'Wenige von denen, die in die Deutsche Bewegung thätig eintraten, mögen gewesen sein, die nicht die Herstellung Polens, innerhalb solcher Grenzen wie sie durch das bereits errungene Uebergewicht der Bevölkerung Deutscher Nationalität auf vormals Polnischem Boden gezogen wurden, für eine Sache der Gerechtigkeit, ja der politischen Weisheit, erachtet haben würden.'

[2] To him truly applies Goethe's *dictum*: 'In der Begrenzung zeigt sich der Meister.'

looked and the conclusions neglected, but the debility of German liberalism can be clearly discerned in those early months of the 'glorious revolution' of 1848, when the professorial lambs at Frankfort, bitten by the Pan-German dog, caught rabies.

XIII

In the *Polenprozess* of August–December 1847, 254 Poles were tried in connexion with the revolutionary plot of the previous year, and over 100 were found guilty.[1] On 20 March the revolution released the prisoners from Moabit gaol, and they were led through the streets in a triumphal procession headed by Miero-sławski and Libelt. In a carriage drawn by the cheering crowd they were taken before the Royal Palace, and the King had to come out and salute them; thence the *Polenzug* proceeded to the University where Mierosławski, waving a Polish and a German flag, harangued the crowd (in French) on the eternal friendship which the two nations should vow to each other, and on their alliance against the common enemy, Russian absolutism. The next day a proclamation by Libelt was posted on the walls of Berlin: 'You feel that the time has come to expiate the fatal deed of Poland's partition, and to safeguard a free Germany by raising the bulwark of an independent Poland against the onset of the Asiatics. . . .'[2] Even at Poznań the Germans at first responded, and on 22 March one of their leaders declared in a speech, subsequently printed as a proclamation to the Poles: '. . . the German nation has spurned the alliance of its Princes with Asiatism, and is ready to carry its flag of Black-Red-Gold, together with yours, into the battle of light against darkness.'[3]

But there was another aspect of the Polish question brought out by the revolution. The Polish National Committee at Poznań announced on 20 March: '. . . the unification of Germany has been proclaimed. . . . We as Poles, a nation apart, cannot agree to being included in it. . . .'[4] And on the 23rd a deputation from Posnania, headed by the Archbishop, presented

[1] See Kieniewicz, op. cit., pp. 78–9.

[2] See Rakowski, op. cit., p. 76, and Hans Schmidt, *Die polnische Revolution des Jahres 1848 im Grossherzogtum Posen* (1912), p. 65. A copy of the poster, 'Dank-Adresse der von Sr. Majestät dem Könige amnestierten Polen an das Berliner Volk', is in P.R.O., F.O. 64/285, No. 73, enclosure in Lord Westmorland's dispatch of 22 Mar. In a proclamation sent by Libelt from Berlin to Poznań, he wrote: 'Here the entire nation has but one desire: that Poland should re-arise as an independent State and form a bulwark against the East' (Rakowski, op. cit., Appendix, pp. 9–10).

[3] Ibid., Appendix, p. 13.   [4] Ibid., Appendix, pp. 10–11.

a petition to the King which declared that when the Germans were about to unite in 'a single State based on the principle of nationality', Posnania was convinced that this was also 'the hour of Poland's resurrection'; they asked for 'a national re-organisation' to be carried through by a local Committee co-operating with a Royal Commissary.[1] The demand was conceded in principle by a 'Cabinet-Order' of 24 March, signed by the King: but both nationalities were to be represented on the Committee, and order and legality were to be maintained in the meantime.[2]

The Poles did not wait. Their National Committee assumed governmental powers, local committees were formed in towns and rural districts, unpopular officials were removed,[3] army camps were started, taxes were levied, volunteers were raised and trained (with the connivance of the Prussian military, who were themselves convinced that war with Russia was imminent).[4] Émigrés were arriving from the west, having been given free passage, or even free transport, across Germany.[5] In places anti-German and anti-Jewish riots broke out, deprecated by the

[1] For the text of the petition, see Rakowski, op. cit., App., pp. 15–16. The immediate task suggested for the Commission was to replace the troops stationed in Posnania by local forces, and imported German officials by residents of the province.

[2] Hepke, op. cit., p. 48. The Cabinet-Order did not enter into the specific demands of the Polish petition; the reply was a compromise arrived at by a Cabinet meeting held during the night of 23–4 Mar., at which the War Minister, von Rohr, demanded the partition of Posnania between Germans and Poles, on the basis of a plebiscite, while Baron von Arnim developed his scheme of using the Poles against Russia (see Kieniewicz, op. cit., p. 108). See also the Ministerial Declaration of 26 Mar., limiting membership of the Commission to natives of Posnania—a further concession to the Poles (Hepke, op. cit., p. 48).

[3] In some places, the officials, supported by the German population, offered successful resistance; for instance, Juncker von Ober-Cornreuth, the Landrat of Czarnikau—see his memoirs, Im Polen-Aufruhr, 1846–48.

[4] See, for instance, Łukomski's Diary, published by K. Rakowski, Dwa pamiętniki z 48 roku (Two Diaries of 1848) (1906); he describes how on 25 Mar., at Sulmierzyce, Lipski, a neighbouring squire, announced that the Germans were fraternizing with the Poles in Berlin, and would let them build up a Polish Army 'in order jointly to conquer Poland's independence'. Some 300 volunteers went into training. One day Prussian troops arrived because of a rumour of anti-German disturbances. The German Colonel, Bonin (afterwards a notorious anti-Pole) thus concluded his address to the Polish volunteers: 'Wir werden vereint gegen den östlichen Feind ziehen' ('We shall march together against the enemy in the East').

[5] The Pre-Parliament passed a resolution expressing the wish 'that the German Governments should grant a free passage, and if necessary support, to Poles returning home without arms'.

Polish leaders, vastly exaggerated by rumour and by German propaganda,[1] and minimized by Polish apologists who had, however, to admit that some such incidents did occur: a bad beginning for the 'fraternal union' of the two nations.

Adolphe de Circourt (not in sympathy either with the Poles or with revolution) reported from Berlin on 29 March 1848:[2]

A week ago, the emancipation of Prussian Poland occurred in fact, and almost in law. Its German population is now a mere accessory, and follows trembling the direction forced on it by the Slav population. The German troops hold a position intermediary between that of hostages and of a foreign Army of Occupation. . . . The Polish Committees formed spontaneously between March 21 and 24, control the administration of the country, and work on reorganising it completely in an exclusively Polish sense. . . . This strange condition of a great province of the Prussian State is, moreover, only the beginning. The Committees have told the King, the Cabinet, the Clubs, and, through the Press, all the inhabitants of the Kingdom that it is their aim to re-establish the Kingdom of Poland. They will transform Posnania into a recruiting centre, a training ground, an arsenal, a supply base.

From here they will invade Russian Poland. They expect help from Galicia, and also the co-operation of Germany, where their influence is considerable among the students and literary men; part of the Press preaches war against Russia. The King told the Poles that he had done for them all that was in his power, but that he could not help them against Russia. Arnim, the Foreign Minister,[3] went farther, and told Circourt that Prussia would do nothing to prevent volunteers, German or foreign,

[1] How successful German 'atrocity propaganda' was even in this country can be seen from the following passage in Theodore Martin's *Life of the Prince Consort* (vol. ii, pp. 70–1): 'Early in April the Poles in Posen rose in revolt, and fell upon their German fellow-subjects with a savage fury which spared neither age nor sex, and vented itself in every species of cruelty and brutal outrage. The customary horrors of war were aggravated by whatever the fiercest passions could suggest.' But Charles Didier (who was friendly to the Poles) wrote to Circourt from Poznań on 10 Apr.: 'Do not believe the news sent from here by the Germans; they detest the Poles, and exaggerate anything which may discredit them. All these murders, all these fires which cause so much noise in Berlin, are pure invention. I have investigated those stories, and found them baseless.'

[2] *Souvenirs d'une mission à Berlin en 1848* (1908), vol. i, pp. 305–10.

[3] It is necessary to distinguish three Arnims: Count von Arnim-Boytzenburg, Prussian Prime Minister, 19–29 Mar. 1848; Baron von Arnim-Suckow, Prussian Ambassador in Paris, 1846–8, and Foreign Minister, 21 Mar.–17 June 1848; and Count von Arnim-Heinrichsdorf, Prussian Ambassador in Vienna, 1845–8 and 1851–8, and Foreign Minister, Feb.–May 1849.

from joining the Poles, though these must not cross Prussia in armed, organized bands: '. . . the principle of the restoration of independent nations for which they will fight, is a just principle' —it is 'our own principle'. It may result in war between Prussia and Russia. The Poles, intimated Arnim, count also on French help. But Circourt in his report expressed doubts whether good relations could long be preserved between the Germans and Poles: whatever the theoretical sympathies of German Liberals, the people felt an invincible dislike of the Poles.

Meyendorff, a most careful observer, wrote on 19 March to Nesselrode about 'the blind hatred unleashed in Germany against Russia';[1] and on the 25th, to Prince Paskevich, Governor-General of Russian Poland:[2]

> The sympathies of the Republican Party for the Polish cause are such that if it prevails . . . war against Russia for the restoration of Poland will follow immediately. If monarchy is saved, it will be surrounded by so many Republican elements that the danger will remain.

But in a letter of the same day to Nesselrode he recommended extreme restraint:

> Surely we do not want to provoke Prussia, nor hurt German feelings; we shall not undertake any hostile act or serious demonstration, but we shall preserve a strictly defensive attitude and leave to our enemies the guilt of aggression.[3]

On 29 March he reports the arrival of numerous Polish *émigrés* from Paris and Brussels.[4] The Prussian Government, fearing their presence in Berlin, wishes them to proceed to Posnania, where

> they will not find the facilities they expect. They will not be able to seize the fortress of Poznań, nor the arms of the *Landwehr*, and the German population of the Grand-Duchy is not favourably disposed to them. These Germans arm against the Poles, and demand aid and protection from the Government . . .
> . . . the Government may possibly regain some force and consistence, and then there will be no war of Prussia against us . . .
> . . . Polish refugees are gathering, and will gather, on our frontier, revolution will be prepared over there, and next, war against us . . . a sort of National Government will be set up, and volunteers will collect from all over the world. People of every class in Posnania will range themselves under that flag: all this would entitle us to declare war on a Government which tolerates such doings, and me, to demand

---

[1] See *Briefwechsel*, vol. ii, p. 49.
[2] Ibid., pp. 52–3.   [3] Ibid., pp. 50–1.   [4] Ibid., pp. 56–8.

my passports, but . . . we must not hasten the break; what I desire most is that we should have to deal with the Poles alone, and not with Prussia, which would drag in Germany against us, and in the end France.

A wise dispatch. Two days later (31 March) Circourt reported to Lamartine[1] that Baron von Arnim had put to him a question which called for a speedy reply: Prussia has let the Poles organize in Posnania; she will not attack Russia; but if the Poles attack, and the Russians occupy Posnania, what will France and England do?

The Prussian Government think that the time has come to ask this question, in a confidential but formal manner, and it is through me [reported Circourt] that they do so to-day. Their decision may, to a high degree, depend on your reply. What do they expect, or rather hope, from you?

Two things: first, a solemn declaration of alliance and political solidarity in matters pertaining to the restoration of Poland; this would give them moral support of appreciable value. Secondly, the despatch, if asked for, of a French squadron to the Baltic.[2] . . . Von Arnim implores you to give weight to the above consideration, and . . . to attach your name to the great and sacred work of Poland's resurrection.

If the French, British, and German nations unite in this enterprise, 'legitimate in its aims, and feasible seeing the formidable strength of such a combination', the fear of war in western and central Europe will disappear—Arnim obviously thought that he was furthering a cause near and dear to the hearts of the French.

On 2 April Lamartine brought the matter before the Provisional Government, and on the 4th his secretary, Comte de Champeaux, informed Circourt that he would 'probably receive no new instructions. . . . It would be rash to build on shifting sand.' But Champeaux had obtained for him the following reply:

'If Russia attacked Prussia and invaded her territory seizing Posnania, France would give Prussia armed support.' You may use this phrase confidentially and in conversation, but you must go no further.

This in reply to Arnim's request for 'a solemn declaration of alliance and political solidarity in matters pertaining to the restoration of Poland'! On 23 May Lamartine, who in the

---

[1] Op. cit., vol. i, pp. 325-8.
[2] Prussia asked for support by sea as they would not have French troops, even as allies, cross Germany—an attitude which resembles that of the Poles towards Russia during the negotiations of Mar.–Aug. 1939.

meantime had left the Foreign Office, defending in Parliament his past policy towards Poland, exclaimed:

Ought we to have forgotten all other relations of France for the sake of that single one, the most sacred, I admit, for it is the most unhappy, but also the most distant, and, under some aspects, the most impossible? . . . Ought we to have forgotten our own frontiers? . . . our own internal difficulties?

Lamartine's Polish policy was sensible, but hardly frank.[1] He had a sound regard for French interests and, it seems, an equally sound distrust of the stability of the new Prussian Government and of its power to carry through a policy of its own. Lastly, he must have soon realized that Great Britain had set her face against any war.

Sir Stratford Canning, on his return journey to Constantinople, was sent by Palmerston to tour the courts of central Europe. On 30 March he had at Potsdam a private interview with Frederick William IV, who confided to him 'the painful anxiety' he experienced with respect to Posnania which was 'but too likely to become the subject of a serious quarrel between this country and Russia'. After that he saw Arnim, and in a confidential dispatch to Palmerston reported on the two talks:[2]

The object of the King in speaking to me about the Grand Duchy of Posen, was to induce me to dissuade Baron d'Arnim, and through him the Cabinet, from persisting in the idea of granting a national army to that Province. The object of Baron d'Arnim in addressing himself to me on the same subject, was to learn what part Her Majesty's Government would probably take if Russia were to occupy or invade the Grand Duchy in consequence of any aggressive proceedings from its inhabitants. . . .

His Majesty's conviction is, that to concede the point in question, would be to ensure the certainty of a War with the Emperor of Russia, who would occupy Posen, and crush the Poles by the mere weight of his immensely superior army.

He is persuaded on the other hand, that if the Polish inhabitants of Posen, on being refused the privilege of a national army, were by means of emissaries or free companies to menace the Russian districts of Poland, his own troops would be sufficient to restrain them.

---

[1] Paul Henry, in an article, 'Le Gouvernement Provisoire et la Question Polonaise en 1848' (*Revue Historique*, vol. clxxviii, Sept.–Oct. 1936), attempts a defence of its Polish policy. Writing while France still professed to have an active interest and policy in Poland, he could not avow Lamartine's true thought: that France could afford neither. His defence is therefore lame and unconvincing.

[2] Stratford Canning to Palmerston, 30 Mar. 1848: P.R.O., F.O., 30/117, No. 7.

Baron d'Arnim and his colleagues appear to overlook every consideration but that of favoring the Poles of the Grand Duchy in their
enterprize for the rescue of Poland from the dominion of Russia. They
are ready to incur the risk of a War with Russia for this object. They
hope eventually to obtain the countenance and support of England.
They reckon with confidence upon having that of France.

The Poles in their present excitement and activity, will, no doubt, under
any circumstances do their best to embroil Prussia with her Northern
neighbour, and arouse their countrymen to a state of insurrection.

In listening to these communications, I have abstained from expressing an opinion, and I have distinctly stated that I can only receive
them unofficially.

I conceive however . . . that the danger may prove on further communication so urgent as to justify me, when I see Baron d'Arnim again,
in endeavouring to divert him from a course of policy, which is opposed
to the King's opinion and shocks his conscience. However agreable
the proposed plan may be to an active and troublesome Party here, it
appears to be fraught with peril to that system of general peace which,
it is well known, is the constant and anxious desire of Her Majesty's
Government to maintain as long as possible in Europe.

On 3 April Canning, in a second private talk with the King,
seems to have dropped his previous restraint, and remarked on
'the inexpediency and danger . . . of including the grant of a
national armament in the separate organisation promised to the
Poles'—nor did he 'neglect the opportunity of confirming His
Majesty in every pacific sentiment'.[1] But he added that he had
no official instructions concerning the Polish question, and that
Lord Westmorland (the British Ambassador in Berlin) was
'exclusively the official channel of communication' between the
two Governments. As for Westmorland, Arnim seems never to
have approached him with a question which he had put with
so much feeling to Circourt, and so much restraint to Stratford
Canning; and in Westmorland's dispatches Arnim appears
merely as 'very much perplexed' by the condition of Posnania,[2]
but assuring the Ambassador of the determination of the
Prussian Government to see both order and peace preserved.[3]

Palmerston's reply to Arnim's question about Poland was
brief and explicit—he wrote to Stratford Canning on 6 April
instructing him[4]

earnestly to recommend the Prussian Government to abstain from any

[1] Ibid., No. 10.
[2] Westmorland to Palmerston, Berlin, 30 Mar. 1848; F.O., 64/285, No. 92.
[3] Same to same, 1 and 6 Apr.; F.O., 64/286, Nos. 97 and 112.
[4] F.O., 30/117, No. 2.

proceeding which could justly be considered by Russia as aggressive, and to avoid as far as possible any measures which might in their consequences lead to aggression on the Russian territory.

Indeed, at no time seems there to have been any doubt as to the British attitude on this point—Meyendorff wrote to Nesselrode on 12 April: 'British diplomacy does all it can to engage the Prussian Government not to give us umbrage, and not to let themselves be driven by Polish clamour.'[1] And on the 8th: 'Sir Stratford Canning is still here and, I believe, gives none but good advice. He is delighted with our moderation and preaches peace to everybody.'[2]

Frederick William IV, though bitterly opposed to the policy of his new Government, did not dare at first openly to work against it, and merely expressed his violent displeasure by sulky withdrawal from business, by fivefold underlinings in his vulgar and incoherent letters, and by double-dealing. On 10 March, fearing an outbreak in Posnania, he had begged the Tsar to move Russian troops closer to the frontier;[3] but on the 23rd he assured the Poles that he had 'implored the Emperor of Russia in no case to intervene'.[4] On 21 April he told von Gerlach 'how he had opposed the formation of the Polish Corps in Posnania . . . and how the Ministers were perfectly crazy on this point'[5]—yet he had agreed; and the same night he wrote to his sister, the Tsaritsa (in a style which with Germans may pass as *bieder* or *treuherzig*): 'I wish lots of rebels crossed into [Russian] Poland. I would trust Prince Paskevich to hang them all within three days.' ('. . . why should Paskevich hang your rebels?' replied the Tsaritsa. 'Do the job yourself, and do not send us any un-

---

[1] *Briefwechsel*, vol. ii, p. 62.

[2] Ibid., p. 67.

[3] Frederick William wrote to Radowitz on 10 Mar. 1848—see P. Hassel, *Joseph Maria von Radowitz* (1905), p. 494: 'In a personal letter I have asked the Emperor Nicholas to let some of his troops move closer to the frontier of Posnania so as to cool a bit their over-heated heads.' And the Tsar wrote to Paskevich, from St. Petersburg, 2/14 Mar. 1848—see Prince Shcherbatov, *General-Feldmarshal Kniaz Paskevich*, vol. vi (1899), pp. 98–9: 'Dear Father-Commander, I have just received a letter from the King of Prussia. . . . He concludes by mentioning rumours . . . that a massacre of all Germans is being prepared in Posnania . . . and asks me to move our troops closer to the frontier; this, he hopes, will immediately sober the people. I cannot refuse his request. . . . But the frontier must not be crossed without my permission.' (Of the 95 letters from the Tsar to Paskevich, published in vol. vi, none is reproduced in the French edition of the work.)

[4] See *Im Polen-Aufruhr, 1846–1848*, Appendix.

[5] *Denkwürdigkeiten aus dem Leben Leopold von Gerlachs*, vol. i, pp. 152–3.

wanted guests'.)[1] When on 18 May the Ministers were pressing on Frederick William a measure which he thought calculated to provoke Russia, he wrote to the Prime Minister, Camphausen:[2]

  . . . *I shall never go* WITH *France against Russia*; not merely because this would be lunacy, but *also because it is wrong*. If I cannot emerge from this pickle (into which I am being brought, God be my witness, *through no fault of* MINE) *I shall abdicate*—sure and true. I have spoken.

But as early as 8 April Meyendorff had thus summed up the situation in a report to Nesselrode: '. . . the Polish question is no longer a *menace*, though it remains for us a source of *annoyances*, intolerable in the long run.'[3] And on the 16th: 'Posnania should not raise in us *fear*, for I know it raises no *hope* in the Poles.'[4] The sharp conflict which had broken out between them and the Germans was working a change in public opinion all over Germany, in the west and south even more rapidly than in Berlin.

Baron von Arnim, because of his seemingly bold initiative, has of recent years been treated by some historians as a man of ideas and character. But his ideas were based on a misconception of German interests and of public opinion in Germany and western Europe;[5] while his conduct was 'disingenuous, shuffling and tricky':[6] he who in March had described the Polish cause as 'just' and 'legitimate', and had tried to draw the western Powers into action likely to result in war with Russia, three or four months later, in a pamphlet, *Frankfurt und Berlin*,[7] recounted how Prussia had had 'to labour *unaided* in combating . . . the perfidious Polish onset against the maintenance of peace in Europe'.[8]

---

[1] See Haenchen, *Revolutionsbriefe, 1848*, pp. 82 and 92.

[2] E. Brandenburg, op. cit., pp. 97–9.

[3] Op. cit., p. 65.

[4] Ibid., pp. 70–1.

[5] One motive behind Arnim's Polish policy undoubtedly was the wish to acquire popularity for Prussia in Germany and in the west: with the help of popularity and war he meant to merge Germany into Prussia. He did not differ much from Bismarck in his aims, only in ability and common sense.

[6] This description of Arnim's conduct over Slesvig-Holstein was given by Palmerston in a dispatch to Lord Bloomfield, on 28 May 1848: see H. C. F. Bell, *Lord Palmerston*, vol. ii, p. 10.

[7] The introduction to the first edition is dated 4 Aug., and to the second, from which I quote, 30 Oct. 1848. The pamphlet was published anonymously, but there seems to be no doubt concerning its authorship.

[8] In the original (p. 19): 'Es musste . . . *allein* den perfiden polnischen Anlauf gegen die Erhaltung des Friedens von Europa . . . mühsam bekämpfen.'

XIV

On 5 March 1848 a meeting of German notables at Heidelberg[1] decided to convene a larger and more representative gathering from all German lands which should arrange for elections to a National Assembly; and they chose a Committee of Seven to prepare the agenda of the so-called Pre-Parliament (*Vorparlament*) and to issue invitations: those were to be addressed to all members of German Estates or Legislatures, and to a number of distinguished men individually. But this raised the question what lands constituted the body politic of Germany? The German Confederation offered the obvious *prima facie* territorial base for a German Constituent Assembly; still, important readjustments were required to make its frontiers conform with the postulates of the 'national awakening' of 1848, the year in which men set out to re-create the world and thought that they could cast off the fetters of history—and indeed should do so, if these impeded the growth of their own nation. When once, during the next creative bout in 1919, a Polish diplomat expounded to me the very extensive (and mutually contradictory) territorial claims of his country, and I inquired on what principle they were based, he replied with rare frankness: 'On the historical principle, corrected by the linguistic wherever it works in our favour.' This was also the canon of the demiurges of 1848.

Of the Habsburg Monarchy only western Austria was included in the German Confederation—Hungary, Transylvania, and Croatia, Lombardy and Venetia, Dalmatia and eastern Istria, Galicia and the Bukovina, were not; but even in western Austria about half the population was non-German: it comprised the Czechs and the Slovenes on the two flanks of the Inner Austrian provinces, and some Italians and Poles on the fringes. Holstein was included in Germany, but not Slesvig, though the two were historically and constitutionally united with each other and with the Danish Crown. Of Prussia's eight provinces, two—East and West Prussia[2] and Posnania—were

---

[1] They were mostly from the south and west: from Baden 21, Württemberg 9, Hesse 7, Bavaria 5, the Prussian Rhineland 4, Nassau 2, Frankfort 2, and from Austria 1—together 51. A short account of the Heidelberg Conference, together with the proceedings of the Pre-Parliament, is given in the (rather misleadingly entitled) *Verhandlungen des Deutschen Parlaments*. Offizielle Ausgabe. Erste Lieferung (1848). It is often quoted, for short, by the name of its editor, Dr. Jucho.

[2] East and West Prussia, at that time, formed one province.

outside the Confederation, an arrangement which supplied her with a European position, parallel to that of Austria: this was convenient while she had, as a Great Power, to act independently of the German Confederation,[1] but not when by 'merging into Germany' she aimed at carrying the maximum weight within it.[2] When on 12 March the invitations to the Pre-Parliament were issued, the inclusion of Slesvig and East and West Prussia was taken for granted; but no invitations were sent to Posnania. Never before 1793 had it been part of a German State, it was lost by Prussia in 1807, and its recovery in 1815 was trimmed with vague reservations in favour of the Poles and their nationality; the peculiar character of the province was, in fact, acknowledged by the King of Prussia in his 'Occupation-Manifesto' of 15 May 1815. Posnania was to the average German a Polish province, but West Prussia was not.

Posnania had in 1848 a population of about 1,335,000. The official census of December 1843, which can be assumed to favour the Germans (and the presence of 'bilinguals' among the Poles gave scope for statistical manipulations) is usually quoted[3] as having enumerated 790,000 Poles, 420,000 Germans, and 80,000 Jews (mostly Germanized). Kohte[4] gives for 1848 the figures of 804,000 Poles, 453,000 Germans, and 81,000 Jews, which show a disproportionate increase of Germans since 1843. Valentin, without quoting his source or calculations, produces the figures of 847,670 Poles, 409,286 Germans, and 76,759 Jews.[5] Hans Schmidt, a Russian German, who tries to keep so straight

---

[1] The arrangement was therefore revived in 1851.

[2] The population of the territories originally included in the German Confederation would have given Austria 190 seats in the Frankfort Parliament, and Prussia only 150. But because of the refusal of Slav, more especially of Czech, constituencies to return members to the German National Assembly, Austria had a representation of only 120 (see W. Schüssler, *Die nationale Politik der österreichischen Abgeordneten im Frankfurter Parlament*, 1913, p. 17); while Prussia, because of the additional territories included in the Federation, finished by returning 198 members (see G. Küntzel, *Briefwechsel zwischen König Fredrich Wilhelm IV und dem Reichsverweser Erzherzog Johann von Oesterreich (1848–50)*, letter from von Boddian to the King, Frankfort, 27 Nov. 1848: 'The Assembly includes 198 Prussians, of whom 50 belong to the Left'). The apportioning of seats was based, in the absence of more recent estimates, on the *Matrikel des deutschen Bundes* of 1819.

[3] See, for instance, report on Posnania submitted by the Committee for Foreign Affairs to the National Assembly on 24 July 1848: *Stenographischer Bericht über die Verhandlungen der deutschen constituierenden Nationalversammlung zu Frankfurt am Main*, vol. ii, p. 1124.   [4] Op. cit., p. 4.

[5] Op. cit., vol. ii, p. 124.

that he sometimes finishes by leaning backwards, thus redistributes the population of 1843: 840,000 Poles, 370,000 Germans, and 80,000 Jews.[1] It seems therefore safe to conclude that in 1848 there were in Posnania considerably more than 800,000 Poles, and certainly less than 500,000 Germans.

The Posnanian Germans were mostly prosperous peasants or of the lower middle class, with a sprinkling of big landowners—the local German intelligentsia was weak, and the German officials were largely recruited from outside. The urban population was still predominantly German[2] or Jewish, but the towns were small: Poznań had in 1838 less than 33,000 inhabitants, and no other town as much as 10,000. Only in the northern and western districts, round Bromberg and Meseritz, and to a less extent in the south, did the Germans form solid majorities. There, on the periphery, the 're-organization' order of 24 March unleashed a veritable storm of 'addresses' demanding separation from the province about to be handed over to the Poles, and inclusion in West Prussia, Brandenburg, or Silesia. 'The day of national freedom is come for all Germany', declared one such manifesto, 'but for us, German inhabitants of Posnania, it is to be a day of enslavement. . . . This is a season for nations to unite, and whoever tries to split them up . . . mistakes his time and its tendencies. . . .'[3] But the Germans of Poznań, who as yet did not suppose that their town could be taken out of the Polish zone, and others similarly situated, were against partitioning the province: concessions (whose range was shrinking rapidly) were to be made to the Poles, but Posnania was to remain part of Prussia. The Posnanian Germans bitterly resented not being invited to Frankfort; they were therefore promptly assured that there was no intention to exclude them from Germany: and their representatives appeared in the Pre-Parliament. Then the Poles protested, calling it presumption to invite them to a German Congress.

The question what territories should send members to the German National Assembly naturally came up immediately when the Pre-Parliament met on 31 March. Conceptions were

---

[1] Op. cit., p. 79.

[2] Many spurious German claims in 1848, and since, were based on this or that town representing German culture, *deutschen Fleiss und deutsche Arbeit*: they anticipated the hysterical Polish propaganda over Lvóv, where a small Polish majority, including imported officials and baptized Jews, was to justify annexing territory with a ten times greater number of autochtonous Ukrainian peasants.   [3] Kohte, op. cit., p. 32.

still crude and doctrinaire, ideas fluid and confused—there had not been time to cover up contradictions with a veneer of plausibility; nor had the first flush of revolutionary enthusiasm and a naively optimistic idealism worn off: none the less, even at this early stage, an aggressive German nationalism began to emerge, as often in speeches by Radicals and Republicans tinged with the *völkisch* element, as by men from the *Ostmarken*, forerunners of 'Prussianism'.

Slesvig was discussed first; its spokesman admitted that there was 'also a Danish population' who looked to Denmark, as much as the Germans to Germany:

> . . . but Slesvig has for centuries been inseparably united with Holstein, and through Holstein with Germany . . . and I trust that this Assembly will loudly and firmly declare that Slesvig . . . should be forthwith received into the German Confederation, and should be represented in the Constituent Assembly by freely chosen deputies.

They did so by all votes but one against.

Next, the inclusion of East and West Prussia was moved. Raveaux, of Cologne, assured the House that there was nothing these two provinces 'more ardently desired than to become part of the German nation'. The proposal was carried without the Poles, more than half the population of West Prussia, having been mentioned.[1] The subject of Posnania was opened up by Junghans (who claimed to be the only representative of '500,000 Germans').[2] 'The Sarmatian knocks at our door, the Russian stands armed at our frontier.' He read out his 'mandate'[3] and concluded: 'If we had not Posnania, we should have to conquer it.' Then a West Prussian gave a display of accuracy, logic, and statesmanship: first, hardly anyone in Posnania desires change (the peasants and agricultural labourers fear the tyranny of the

---

[1] In the subsequent debate on Posnania their existence was incidentally acknowledged by Welcker, when he pleaded for self-determination; and in the last sitting of the Pre-Parliament, Truskoski, from West Prussia, spoke about them in a hesitant and oblique manner, and drew a sharp reply from a West-Prussian German.

[2] But in the list of the Pre-Parliament, there appear other Germans from Posnania: Eckert and Roquette (member and deputy member for Bromberg —Wirsitz in the Frankfort Parliament), and Dr. Fürst, a native of Poznań, resident in Leipzig. They may have arrived after the opening of the session.

[3] Its terms are not given either in Jucho, or Kohte, or Hepke, or in Bleck, 'Die Posener Frage auf den National-Versammlungen in den Jahren 1848 und 1849 (*Zeitschrift der Historischen Gesellschaft für die Provinz Posen*, vol. xxix).

Polish gentry, and 'the landowners and towns are completely German'); secondly, a demarcation line between the Poles and Germans can be drawn, which the Poles should in fairness accept; but thirdly, the German frontier should not be fixed, as war with Russia is likely and, if victorious, the Germans may in a few weeks reach a line from Lake Peipus to the Black Sea. 'Our frontiers were drawn by the sword—leave them also for the future to the sword.' And Gustav von Struve, of Mannheim, one of the 'Reds' of 1848, argued thus:

> . . . we cannot abandon the 700,000 Germans of Posnania. This would be betraying our German brethren. . . . We summon the German inhabitants of Posnania to the German Constituent Assembly. While doing so, we must express what the Germans feel about the unholy dismemberment of Poland. We declare it our sacred duty to repair the wrong, as far as this can be done without injustice to those Germans.

Two speakers were staunchly idealistic—first, Leisler from Nassau:

> Those who desire to be free, must . . . be just. . . . They who have committed a tort must repay the debt in full, and retain no profit. . . . Gentlemen, when did we first rob Poland? In 1772. Therefore Poland must be reconstituted in the frontiers of 1772. . . . This will obviously create a difficult position for the German inhabitants [of Posnania]. . . . They have to be compensated by the German nation.

And next, Hensel from Saxony:

> It has been pointed out that there are 500,000 Germans in Posnania. Admitted: and even were there yet another 500,000, I should still say that justice must prevail rather than prudence. . . .

(But neither speaker noticed that the frontiers of 1772 comprised also West Prussia which, no less than Posnania, raised a problem both of restitution and of national justice.)

Welcker, a learned and high-minded Liberal from Baden, appealed to 'the great principles of nationality and liberty', and pleaded for self-determination.

> We do not want to apportion countries like acres. . . . I want Poland to be restored. But we ourselves have lost Alsace and Lorraine. We shall not rashly give away everything. Or we, too, shall have to reclaim what we have lost.

Venedey, of Cologne, supplied a Radical brand of *Realpolitik*:

> It would be unjust and unwise to encroach on Poland. Is Poland to be with us or against us? If a single Pole doubts our sympathy, they will be against us. . . . Russia's vanguard. . . . We do not want Posnanian deputies in our Assembly.

In the end the Pre-Parliament recognized that in its lopsided, haphazard composition[1] it had, if possible, to avoid pronouncing judgement on vital issues acknowledged as controversial: it was decided to summon members from the territories included in the German Confederation, and from Slesvig and East and West Prussia, while leaving the question of Posnania to the National Assembly; but a resolution was carried declaring the dismemberment of Poland a 'shameful wrong', and her restoration 'a sacred duty of the German nation'. Before the Pre-Parliament adjourned on 3 April, the admission of Posnanian Germans to the National Assembly was demanded once more. Roquette, from Bromberg, spoke with ominous passion: 'We are Germans, and want to remain Germans . . . we love the Poles as neighbours, not as brothers . . . we are not Poles, but Germans, and you cannot, and must not, abandon us.'

The Radicals wished the Pre-Parliament to continue till the National Assembly had met, but the majority decided to set up a Committee of Fifty (*Fünfziger-Ausschuss*) to carry on together with the Federal Diet, now representing Governments refurbished by revolution.

On 6 April the Prussian Provincial Estates met for a last session. Those of Posnania, after a heated debate, rejected inclusion in Germany by 26 Polish against 17 German votes; whereupon the German minority, acting independently, elected five members to represent the northern and western districts in the Frankfort Parliament. But on the 7th the Federal Diet, endorsing a resolution of the Pre-Parliament, declared for elections by constituencies, which were bound to produce even sharper conflicts where resisted by a non-German population.

XV

In March far-reaching concessions and promises were made to the Poles by the King and the Prussian Government, who, stunned by what was happening in the streets of Berlin, had for

---

[1] Even in the Pre-Parliament the south-west and west were greatly over-represented: from Hesse-Darmstadt there were 84 representatives, from the other three Hessian States 54; from Baden 72; from Württemberg 52; and from Frankfort 12—together 274 in a total of 521 (in the Frankfort Parliament these States had 79 in a total of about 600 members). Further, of 141 Prussians at least 100 were from the Rhineland and the adjoining districts of Westphalia, and of 44 Bavarians, at least 13 were from the Rhenish Palatinate. Thus more than three-fourths of the Pre-Parliament were from western or south-western Germany, from the Rhine or the Lower Main, regions which the legend of 1848 credits with a most touching 'liberal' idealism. There were only two Austrians in the Pre-Parliament.

a while lost touch with political realities outside the heaving, convulsed centres of revolution: gliding into the void, they obeyed naive, irrelevant behests with regard to Poland which reached them from the void. Had the revolutionary forces been powerful and enduring, they might have created a new reality and evolved a coherent policy of their own, of which an attempt to solve the Polish question would have been part and parcel: being local, transient, and divided, they merely burdened the remote and complex problem of Posnania with a heritage of contradictions and confusion. The administration was to be Polonized, and Polish armed forces were being formed: but unless the movement found vent in a revolutionary war against Russia, it was bound, confined to Posnania, to unload itself in a local conflict between the Poles and Germans, which in turn was bound to destroy any incipient German-Polish alinement in international affairs. At first Germans and Poles alike had viewed Posnanian developments from the angle of imminent war in the east—what sense would there otherwise have been in admitting Russian-Polish *émigrés* to the armed camps in Posnania, and, indeed, in facilitating their journey across Germany? But the forces in Great Britain and France, and also in Russia, which had prevented the February Revolution from ushering in a European war, were at work once more to immunize the March Revolution in international relations. The Poles, who as a nation had nothing to lose and everything to gain in a revolutionary European war, were playing a pathetically hopeless game against the western Powers which, from a determination to preserve the peace of Europe, had turned anti-revolutionary. The course of international politics quickly circumscribed the Posnanian movement within its provincial borders, and the subsequent developments gave a powerful impulse to counter-revolutionary nationalism in Germany.

In Posnania the Prussian military were counter-revolutionary and anti-Polish, and so were most of the officials, while even the revolutionary ferment among its German population was assuming an aggressively nationalist, anti-Polish character: they felt indignant at the Government promises to the Poles given 'without consulting the province'.[1] 'We shall defend our German national character with the same courage which Berlin has shown', wrote on 4 April S. G. Kerst, a secondary school-teacher at Meseritz (and its representative at Frankfort where he joined the Left Centre). And on the 2nd: '. . . the attitude

[1] Kerst in the Frankfort Parliament, 26 July 1848.

(*Stimmung*) of the public in towns and villages exceeds by far all our expectations.'[1] Round Bydgoszcz (Bromberg) the Germans started organizing a *Freicorps*.[2] 'A powerful *Volksgeist* had been awakened', wrote in retrospect Hepke, another German schoolmaster from Posnania; 'everywhere Citizens' Committees were formed. . . . The German cause was at stake.'[3] The *Volksgeist* of mass-movements replaced the *Zeitgeist* of the intellectuals, and came to be worshipped by the modern *clercs*.[4] '*Deutsche Männer und Freunde!*'[5] thundered Professor Mittermaier of Heidelberg, President of the Pre-Parliament, in his opening speech, '. . . The giant is awakening. The *Volksgeist* is that giant. He is awake.'

On the Polish side, too, the masses were stirring, and the Polish National Commission 'suddenly found itself at the head of a movement which it could not control'.[6] The outlook, aims, and reactions of those masses were narrowly provincial, and while the leaders and the upper classes were thinking foremost of the wider aspects of the Polish question and of Poland's integral restoration, armed Posnanian peasants or *petit bourgeois* were turning against the local Germans, against the officials at whose hands they had suffered a good deal, and against the Jews: rumours circulated that 'the Holy Father has given permission to kill the Prussians', and that 'the time has come to pilfer the Jews'. In fact the movement might ultimately have assumed even a socially radical character. Count Działyński wrote on 27 March to Herr von Minutoli, President of Police in Berlin:[7]

The troops will succeed wherever they go, but their successes will cost the lives of the German inhabitants, next those of the Jews, and in the end of all the gentry. The only way of saving the situation is by forming Polish regiments under General von Willisen: the disorder has to be organised.

Wilhelm von Willisen, a staff officer of high standing and great erudition and repute, had spent nine years in Posnania, 1832–41, was a trusted friend of the Poles, and in the early days of the revolution discussed with Mierosławski plans for war against Russia. The Poles desired to see him placed in charge of 'national reorganization', and, after an initial refusal, the

[1] Kohte, op. cit., p. 37.   [2] Rakowski, op. cit., App., p. 67.
[3] Hepke, op. cit., p. 17.
[4] For these see Julien Benda's brilliant book, *La Trahison des clercs* (1927).
[5] Those who know the Germans squirm at such heartiness—*deutsche Biederkeit*—which the novelist, Arthur Schnitzler, a Vienna Jew, has correctly defined as *ein Gemisch von Stumfsinn und Tücke* ('a compound of obtuseness and treachery').
[6] Rakowski, op. cit., p. 107.   [7] Kohte, op. cit., p. 52.

Government decided to send him as Royal Commissary to Posnania: he was to start work on Polonizing the province while safeguarding Prussia's sovereignty, and to try to induce the Polish National Committee to keep their hands off the German districts;[1] and, last but not least, he was to seek, through voluntary disbanding, a settlement of (what now would be called) the Polish 'private army'.

This army was concentrated in four camps, and by the beginning of April was approaching 10,000;[2] primarily raised for war against Russia, they also 'burnt with a desire to fight the Prussians'.[3] Against them, the Prussian Army Command, by summoning troops and *Landwehr* from the neighbouring provinces, had gathered forces much superior in number and armament, and burning with a single-minded hatred of the Poles:[4] by the beginning of April General von Colomb, G.O.C. Poznań, had over 20,000 men at his disposal. He longed to take strong action against the Poles—wherein he was encouraged by the King but restrained by the Government. On 1 April he was told by order from the War Minister that 'the revolutionaries, not only everywhere in Germany, but throughout the world, are interested in the restoration of Poland', and that he must therefore avoid stern action which would cost Prussia 'all sympathies'.[5] But two days later the King, through his A.D.C., instructed Colomb to use all means at his disposal for the restoration of 'order and obedience in the province'; to which the significant remark was added that 'scenes such as happened in Galicia, should not occur'.[6]

[1] See Ministerial Memorandum of 30 Mar., in Willisen, *Akten und Bemerkungen über meine Sendung nach dem Grossherzogtum Posen im Frühjahr 1848* (1850), p. 15.

[2] Willisen quotes higher figures, but according to Rakowski, the Poles, to impress him with their strength, had exaggerated to him their numbers.

[3] Rakowski, op. cit., p. 123.

[4] See ibid., App., p. 33, for anti-Polish song of the Prussian *Landwehr*— their anger, like that of the Paris National Guard before the June Days, was exacerbated by their having to give up their ordinary occupations, with great inconvenience to themselves. The last stanza of that doggerel ran thus:

> 'Drum Pollakei, fass dich jetzt kurz,
> Mach' dich gefasst auf ew'gen Sturz;
> Denn Polen darf nicht frei mehr sein,
> Wenn wir uns woll'n der Ruh' erfreu'n.'

[5] See O. Hoetzsch, 'Die Stellung des Generals von Colomb zur Revolution in Posen und zu Willisen', in the *Zeitschrift für Osteuropäische Geschichte* (1914), p. 366.

[6] Ibid., p. 343. Apparently the King did expect Colomb to use the

The orders with which Willisen started on his mission were similarly contradictory and ambiguous, and those subsequently sent to him from Berlin were no less vague: which perhaps did not trouble him at first, as it left him greater latitude. Nor did he, in his eagerness to succeed, hold the same language to the various parties: he would interpret the same transaction to each in the way which he expected to render it acceptable. In the nature of things, his mission was foredoomed to failure: the basis of the new policy had vanished before he ever set out. But exaggerated hopes had been raised among the Poles, and exaggerated fears among the Posnanian Germans, who received Willisen with hostility and distrust; from the very outset, he had been denied control of the military, and he was sabotaged by the civil administration, who sometimes went the length of openly defying his orders. 'It is not clear', writes a German historian, 'whether the authorities had secret directions to work against him, or whether they did so spontaneously, while pursuing their official routine.'[1]

He arrived in Poznań on 5 April, having crossed a countryside as still and tense as if it had been no-man's land between hostile armies. The next day he issued an address to Poles and Germans, which satisfied neither; moreover, he did so before having met Colomb. When he called on the General,[2] he found that Colomb was about to attack the Polish camps; and Willisen had the utmost difficulty to obtain a few days' respite in which to attempt an understanding. On the 6th, at night, Willisen wrote to the Minister of the Interior, von Auerswald: 'Conditions here have become completely anarchical; Government authority reaches no further than the military can enforce it.... The military are set on using force.' Unless otherwise instructed from Berlin, Colomb will attack the Poles on 10 April.[3] Willisen proposed (to use Działyński's expression) to organize disorder by forming the Polish forces, much reduced in number, into a distinct Polish unit within the Prussian army.

peasants against the gentry, but avoid a *jacquerie*: the remark which he made to the Polish deputation on 23 Mar., claiming for the Prussian administration the merit of having prevented a repetition of the Galician 'scenes' in Posnania, suggests that the *faux bonhomme* was playing with the idea.

[1] See R. Bartolomaeus, op. cit., pp. 13–14.

[2] From Willisen's papers it would appear that he called on Colomb on the 6th; Colomb gives the date of the 7th. There seems to have been an initial *contretemps* complicated by punctilios of etiquette; there certainly was mutual dislike and distrust.

[3] See Willisen, op. cit., pp. 21–2.

His suggestion was disallowed from Berlin (the King subsequently told Colomb that from the very outset he had 'clearly ordered' Willisen not to leave the Poles 'a single armed man').[1] But on 8 April Colomb was told by the Minister for War to give, if necessary, military support to Willisen 'who is instructed to start work on Polish national reorganisation' (as if this could have been done before the problem of the camps was settled); and further that 'it would be highly embarrassing for the Government' if Willisen 'found himself compelled to relinquish his task'. The same day, the King wrote to Colomb regretting that his operations should have suffered delay, and telling him to act should Willisen fail to disarm the Poles.[2]

It was under such conditions that the negotiations were conducted. The Polish leaders realized that a collision with the Prussian troops would spell disaster for their forces and for any political hopes they might still entertain. They therefore concluded with Willisen on 11 April the so-called Jarosławiec Agreement: the Polish forces, reduced to less than 3,000, were to be formed into a Posnanian division, with the Polish flag and colours and language of command; the rest were to be disbanded, deserters from the Prussian forces to be pardoned, while foreigners (mostly Russian Poles) were to be removed, but not to be delivered to their Governments. By now it was not so much Poland as 'order' which was being restored. But as a corollary to it, 'national reorganization' was promised once more: the Polish language in schools, offices, and law-courts, and Polish officials in control of the administration; and Willisen, claiming to have re-established order, now meant to proceed with the task. The Posnanian Germans howled with anger and indignation.

The imminent 'reorganization' forced the issue of partition, and on 14 April a Cabinet Order was published that it 'must not extend to parts in which the German population predominates'. A line was drawn cutting off the northern and western districts with 593,900 inhabitants: over 100,000 more than the total German population of the province. While the most reasonable among the Poles would have been prepared to cede a few genuinely German districts if at that price they could have retained the friendship of the German national movement, against such a partition the Polish National Committee was bound to protest, and protest in earnest. But when on 22 April

[1] Hoetzsch, op. cit., p. 344. But the King was notoriously untruthful.
[2] Ibid., pp. 344-5.

the Prussian representative moved in the Federal Diet that these districts 'bordering on federal territory . . . should, in accordance with the wishes of their inhabitants, be received into the German Confederation', the resolution was carried unanimously, most of the other Governments, more advanced in German nationalism than Prussia, merely regretting that the town and fortress of Poznań was not included in the German zone.[1] When on the night of 19 April Willisen returned to Poznań, at the city gate, by order from Colomb, he was refused admission on the ground that his presence in the town might produce a breach of the peace: the G.O.C. professed himself unable to guarantee the safety of the Royal Commissary against the anger of the German population! Willisen immediately left Posnania. Looking back the enlightened Prussian nobleman wrote in 1850: 'The manner in which the violent opposition of the Germans developed against what they understood by "national reorganization", for the first time placed before my eyes a picture of passionate excitement among the masses incapable of wider political conceptions.'[2]

The day before the Jarosławiec Agreement was signed, Prussian troops attacked a Polish detachment near Tremeszna; other encounters followed. In granting the Poles an army unit of their own, Willisen had exceeded his authority; and neither the Prussian military nor the Polish commander, Mierosławski, who had evaded appending his signature to the agreement, meant to honour it. The Polish forces were scattering, disappointed and discontented, and even where they did not cause trouble, their presence supplied the Germans with a welcome excuse. 'I ordered the mobile columns to attack the insurgents at all points', writes Colomb in his 'Memorandum' on 1848.[3] Starting with 19 April a series of pitched battles was fought, in two of which, on 30 April and 2 May, the Germans were routed. Willisen's successor, General von Pfuel, a pro-Russian agreeable to the King and the Army Command, wrote from Poznań on 4 May: 'The province is in complete uproar . . . this is an armed national rising.'[4] But it was bound to collapse—and Mierosławski resigned his command in time for his successor to sign the Polish capitulation (9 May).

. [1] See Kohte, op. cit., p. 72; further Meyendorff's letter to Nesselrode of 25 Apr.: 'According to what Arnim has just told me, the Diet insists on the town and fortress of Poznań remaining German'; *Briefwechsel*, vol. ii, p. 80.

[2] Willisen, op. cit., p. 25.

[3.] Hoetzsch, op. cit., p. 347.   [4] Kohte, op. cit., p. 105.

XVI

On 26 April Posnania came up for discussion in the Committee of Fifty,[1] in an atmosphere very different from that of 31 March. Ideas had lost their revolutionary fluidity; conditions and developments were examined with growing realism and prudence. Declarations of sympathy with Poland, being part of the revolutionary routine, were repeated, but with waning warmth and conviction, and with a touch of weariness. A national egotism, sometimes naive and sometimes cynical, was rising to the surface. Russia was still the enemy, but an attack by her was no longer thought imminent, nor war with her unavoidable. On the other hand fighting had broken out between the Germans and Poles, and there was the *fait accompli* of the partition: of eighteen speakers in the debate, only four spoke directly or by implication against it, objecting not so much to the claims of the Posnanian Germans as to the time and method chosen for gratifying them.

The tone of the debate was set by the *rapporteur* of the subcommittee for Foreign Affairs, Pagenstecher (Rhine-Province). The Polish question, difficult and complex, was 'a heritage of the perfidious politics of past centuries'. The Pre-Parliament 'had dwelt exclusively on Germany's guilt'—but the Poles were not without blame. None the less, Germany wished them to recover their country and independence. But were Prussian Poland set free now, it would succumb to Russia,[2] while Germany, preoccupied with her own reorganization, could not, for the sake of Poland, risk war. Moreover, the Posnanian Germans 'have as good a claim to our sympathy as the Poles'. It is not a question whether Poland is to be restored, but when and how? The problem must be left to the German National Assembly. He warned the Poles not to fan civil war in Posnania.

Of the pro-Poles, Reh (Darmstadt) and Venedey repeated that justice rather than prudence should prevail, but in this case (luckily) the two coincided (judgement seems even more pliable than morals). Schuselka, a Bohemian German (who by setting free the Poles wished to detach them from the Czechs and to

---

[1] *Verhandlungen des Deutschen Parlaments.* Zweite Lieferung (1848), pp. 372–401.

[2] This argument was not devoid of foundation; thus, for instance, Meyendorff wrote to Nesselrode on 8 Apr.: 'It is not impossible that Prussia may declare the independence of the Polish part of Posnania, and then we could occupy it without war with Prussia or Germany' (op. cit., vol. ii, p. 66). See also below, p. 89, n. 3.

lighten 'the Slav burden of Austria'[1]) deplored that a few weeks after the Pre-Parliament had stigmatized the dismemberment of Poland, a new partition should have been effected: frontier rectifications should not be made till the two nations 'faced each other, great and free'. Similarly, Robert Blum (Leipzig), a man of rare sincerity and frankness, argued that it requires free nations to negotiate: the enslaved can only be despoiled. 'It pains me that the young days of our national ascent and the spring-time of our liberty should add such a page to history.' But the argument about 'a nation in fetters', however impressive, was hardly practical politics: the German districts of Posnania could not be expected, for the sake of spiritual elegance, to submit to Polish national reorganization; what could have been expected was some measure of fairness in drawing the demarcation line—and of this there was no longer a chance.

The point reached by German public opinion was thus summed up by Jacoby (Koenigsberg): '. . . all seem agreed that, with the most careful regard for German interests, an independent Poland should be restored.' 'German interests' were rapidly becoming the major premise, offering considerable scope for further developments and embroidery. The conflict in Posnania now engrossed attention, and war with Russia, especially over Poland, was no longer considered in the German interest. There was enough trouble in the north, west, and south, argued Schleiden (Slesvig)—war with Denmark, danger from France, a republican rising in Baden—'is this a time to provoke a new enemy?' The Pre-Parliament had shown 'supreme tact', when it carefully limited itself to proclaiming 'our sympathy which in time will bear fruit'. Von Closen (Munich):

---

[1] In a pamphlet published in 1846, *Deutschland, Polen und Russland*, he wrote (p. 141): 'Without Galicia there would be in Austria 10 million Slavs against 7 or 8 million Germans. Seeing the difference in their cultural level, the position would be decidedly favourable to the Germans, and for that reason alone Austria should have refrained from robbing Poland.' A year later, in his *Oesterreichische Vor- und Rückschritte*, he urged giving up Galicia, and, having declared that for the Czechs it was 'a historic, political, and spiritual necessity to remain connected with Germany, and probably to dissolve completely in the German element', launched out into a violent diatribe against them (see pp. 272–95). He continued preaching his doctrines in 1848. Smolka, in a letter to his wife, dated 20 June 1848, reports a speech by Schuselka describing the inclusion of Galicia in the Austrian Empire as a great mistake, because it created a Slav majority; a position analogous to that of Hungary should be conceded to Galicia, and, at a suitable moment, the province should be handed over to a united, independent Poland, allied to Austria and Germany (*Dziennik*, p. 288).

'We are here to transact German business'; declarations about Poland are philanthropy, and international complications should be avoided. Kierluff (Mecklenburg): 'I wish the German people would for once voice sympathy for German interests, after having so long voiced its enthusiasm for Poland.' Wiesner (Vienna): 'Moderate your noble zeal for Poland!' Jürgens (a Lutheran pastor from Brunswick): '. . . sympathy for a foreign nation, however well-founded and deserved, must not turn into sottishness (*Blödsinn*), which it would be if it went the length of injustice to one's own country and nation.' And Heckscher (Hamburg) wished for a free Poland, but one which would not encroach on German territory or rights; nor should the slavery of a gentry régime be re-created, nor a Galician massacre be repeated. While Polish claims to the whole of Posnania and to West Prussia, or even protests against the unfairness of the demarcation line of 14 April, were rejected as scandalous, new German territorial claims were raised. Abegg (Breslau), Biedermann (Leipzig), and Buhl (Baden) contended that Poznań, because of its strategic importance, should, for the time being, be retained by Prussia; Kierluff protested against the arrangement being treated as temporary: 'the fortress of Poznań is the key to the heart of Germany.' Wedemeyer (Brandenburg) supplied his own version of 'justice': 'Poznań's population is predominantly German, and it must therefore remain with Prussia'; Poland has arisen and has perished by conquest, and what she receives is due to German 'magnanimity': 'the Poles should gratefully accept whatever we give them.'

The Committee of Fifty finished by restating the resolutions of the Pre-Parliament which, while leaving the settlement of Posnania to the National Assembly, condemned the dismemberment of Poland and demanded her restoration as an independent State; but a significant rider was added which, in contorted yet emphatic language, declared that the resolutions of the Pre-Parliament in favour of Poland must not be taken to imply anything which might jeopardize German interests.

While the Fifty talked, the question of Poznań was being settled. On 25 April Meyendorff reports to Nesselrode having been shown a new partition line which assigned the town to Germany: 'The Poles will be left to shout, a resolution will be obtained from the Fifty, after that from the Diet, and then there will be nothing more to worry about.'[1] The next day the new line was published in Berlin, and on 2 May was confirmed by

[1] Op. cit., vol. ii, pp. 79–80.

the Federal Diet: 'On the motion of Prussia, the town and fortress of Poznań, with a district which secures its connexion with Germany, and a population of 273,000, is received into the Germanic Federation.' Thus for a population of less than 500,000, Germany assigned to herself territory with 867,000 inhabitants, while leaving to the Poles, for a population of considerably more than 800,000, territory with 468,000 inhabitants (German 'magnanimity' expressed itself in inverting proportions).[1] But a new promise was added that national reorganization was to start immediately in the part assigned to the Poles. Robert Blum compared the procedure to 'cutting out the heart and then saying: "Now live" '.

Even the line of 2 May did not fully satisfy the Posnanian Germans. On 29 April the Committee called on all communes wishing to appeal against the demarcation line, to supply data, and on the others to specify what safeguards were deemed necessary under Polish reorganization. The years 1918–20 could hardly improve on the variety of arguments now advanced to bolster up further territorial demands: historic rights and 'cultural' claims, economic or strategic considerations, the alleged wishes of a mixed population, the national character of this or that (passionately cherished) town or of the big landed estates, the need to preserve intact the system of roads and railways, &c. On 12 May General von Pfuel drew a third demarcation line, and on 4 June a fourth, each more disadvantageous to the Poles; and he offered to facilitate, by sale or exchange, transfers of landowners between the German and the Polish zones—population transfer in terms of an agrarian community.

On 30 April the Polish National Committee at Poznań announced its own dissolution in a pathetic, but halting and badly written, Manifesto:[2]

When the voice of freedom which inspired the nations of Europe reached our frontiers, the Poles of the Grand Duchy of Poznań thought that for them too the hour of freedom and independence had struck . . . the sympathies of the free nations had aroused the greatest enthusiasm among the Poles. . . . It was in the midst of such enthusiasm that the National Committee was elected.

Fraternal feelings and sympathies being shown by other nations, more especially by the Germans, and even by those who live among

[1] Seeing that half of 867,000 is 438,500, and that certainly more than 50,000 Germans lived in the districts left to the Poles, there must have been a Polish majority within the territory assigned to Germany by the demarcation line of 2 May.

[2] Published in Rakowski, op. cit., App., pp. 57–8.

us, .he National Committee did not, and could not, desire war with
Germany . . ., but alliance and friendship. . . .

After the last hope has vanished of truth and justice prevailing
against calumny and violence, the National Committee recognises that
it cannot, without treason against its countrymen and history, continue
negotiating with the Government, for they will do nothing for the
cause of Poland. . . .

The National Committee dissolves, but hopes that the promises given
to the people will be kept, and that the [Re-organisation] Committee,
entrusted with the work, will continue to function.

The Committee protests solemnly to all Europe against the acts of
violence which have been perpetrated, and lays down its mandate,
which was to promote our cause by justice and not by violence. Force
has destroyed our mandate.

Here was the end of the dream, of the vision, and of the *Polen-
rausch* (the pro-Polish 'intoxication'). When on 4 May the Committee of Fifty for the last time discussed Polish affairs, Venedey
declared: 'Our Committee is no longer the same: at least, for
some time past, it has not acted in the spirit of the Pre-Parliament.' But Jürgens argued: 'The position has changed; previous premises no longer hold good, conditions in Posnania are
different, the Poles have not behaved as was expected.'

The game was up. Some of the chief leaders left Posnania.
The centre of Polish endeavours once more shifted to Paris.
There, in a void, *émigrés* continued to talk and to scheme. Under
date of 15 May, Senior recounts[1] a typical conversation with a
Pole, the wife of Léon Faucher (subsequently Minister of the
Interior under Louis-Napoleon), and sister of Wołowski, a
refugee of 1831, naturalized in France, and in 1848 a prominent
member of the French Parliament:

> She talked politics after the fashion of the Poles—demanding English
> and French intervention to drive the Russians out of Poland. Prussia
> and Austria, she said, would willingly give up their own shares, and the
> old kingdom might be reconstructed as a barrier to Russia. . . . I
> admitted that if any country was ever justified in rising against its
> existing Governments, Poland is the one; . . . but that I could not
> believe that it was in the interest of England or of France to make war
> on Russia in order to assist her. On which she was very angry with my
> egoism.

Under pressure from the Left and the pro-Poles, Lamartine
had to feign diplomatic activity. On 7 May Circourt was instructed to complain of the obstacles offered to the return of

---

[1] *Journals in France and Italy, 1848–1852*, vol. i, pp. 94–5.

Polish *émigrés* (of whom France wished to be rid), and of the disappointing developments in Posnania—after a beginning had been made with the restoration of Polish nationality 'which events would have helped to grow and develop in a manner advantageous to Germany, and offensive to no one' ('sans caractère offensif pour personne').[1] Arnim, not troubled about what he had said six weeks earlier,[2] replied that it had never been intended 'to let the entire Polish emigration establish itself in the Grand-Duchy of Posen, but only natives of the province', for such a gathering would have involved Prussia in war with Russia. 'It was never her intention to engage in such a war', of which, 'were it to break out, Poland would most certainly and most irrevocably be the victim.' At home Prussia is engaged in carrying out her undertakings in whatever genuinely Polish territory she holds, but 'she recognises neither an obligation nor a right to interfere beyond her own frontiers'. Lastly, she has obligations towards the German population of Posnania and of the adjoining provinces, towards Prussia as a whole, and towards the German Confederation, by whose decisions she is bound with regard to delimitations of federal territory.

Prussia passed the buck, and the German National Assembly at Frankfort (*wehmütig* remembered by the 'good Germans' and their foreign friends for nearly a century) disposed of the matter in the *Polendebatte* of July 1848.

XVII

The position of the twelve members from Posnania came up in the National Assembly during the examination of returns; the two resolutions of the Federal Diet of 22 April and 2 May adjudicating upon a matter which the Pre-Parliament had re-served for the decision of the National Assembly, formed the basis of their election; and their full reception into the Assembly would imply the inclusion of their constituencies in the German Confederation. On 5 June the Assembly decided to admit them provisionally to its deliberations, while referring the problem of Posnania to the Committee for Foreign Affairs. This reported on 24 July, the debate occupied the sessions of the 24th, 25th, and 26th, and the voting, with some additional dis-cussions, took place on the 27th. A long distance had been

---

[1] See Lamartine, *Trois mois au pouvoir*, pp. 247–9.
[2] Cf. above, pp. 61–3.

covered since the debate in the Pre-Parliament on 31 March, and even in the Committee of Fifty on 26 April. The Polish armed movement had been beaten down, and the idea of going to war with Russia over Poland had completely vanished. German public opinion, by and large, had turned against the Poles, while in France the revolutionary forces, which had inscribed Poland on their banners, had been crushed. Counterrevolution was advancing, both in Germany and all round her. The national reorganization of Posnania, proclaimed in the fervour of the March revolution, and meant as the first step towards an integral restoration of Poland, had territorially been whittled down to a diminutive 'Duchy of Gnesen' and was to be paid for by the inclusion of almost two-thirds of Posnania in Germany: that is, by a disruption, and a virtual destruction, of Prussian Poland. The endeavours of Poles and pro-Poles were now concentrated on preserving an undivided Posnania within the framework of Prussia; they were fighting a delaying action. Still, the outcome was a foregone conclusion: the *fait accompli* of the partition, the inclusion and the consequent elections, could hardly be undone in an atmosphere of rising nationalism, and the interest of the debate is psychological rather than pragmatic. It is a milestone on the road traversed by the German revolution of 1848.

The Report of the Committee, adopted by all votes against one (Schuselka's), assumes the garb of scholarship; among its authors were historians of rank, such as Gervinus,[1] von Raumer,

---

[1] Gervinus, in March a strong pro-Pole, began to veer round early in April, and openly recanted his previous views in a leading article in the *Deutsche Allgemeine Zeitung*, on 19 Apr.: the Poles were to be taught that 'it was not fear but magnanimity which had actuated' the Germans in their offers (see Feldman, op. cit., pp. 172–3). E. M. Arndt, another member of the Committee for Foreign Affairs (whom the Radical of 1848, Venedey, describes as 'the good, old German conscience', and the neo-Liberal Veit Valentin, as '*diese prächtig-wunderliche Persönlichkeit*'—see op. cit., vol. ii, p. 13) was less frank but even more forcible in his language. He who in 1843 had advocated the creation of a Polish *Mittelreich* between Germany and Russia (see above, p. 49), now in a leaflet *Polenlärm und Polenbegeisterung (Noise and Enthusiasm about the Poles)*, talked about the *Polennarren* (pro-Polish sots), and classified them under the three headings of 'blockheads', 'fools', and 'scoundrels'. He declared: 'Never and nowhere have I held out high and splendid hopes for the Poles or for a great Poland', and he denied the Slavs creative political or intellectual abilities—'the Russians form an honourable exception . . . they have an admixture of the Germanic Scandinavians . . .', and also the Czechs who have much *urdeutsches*. Clearly the distance between these '48-ers' and the modern German 'racialists' is not overgreat.

and Stenzel, and several distinguished jurists. Having analysed the history of Posnania, especially since 1815, and the position created by the revolution, it proceeds to contrast the national with the territorial principle. 'The Germans in the Grand-Duchy thought about the Poles, not about the land.' They wished to do justice to the Polish nationality, but not to be themselves separated from Germany 'at a time when the German national feeling is running stronger than ever before'. 'The Germans say: "the soil is neither Polish nor German, only the inhabitants determine its national character." They are German to the core, want to remain it, and to belong to Germany. They ask to be received into the German Confederation.' 'Germans could not force other Germans at the point of the bayonet to submit to a Polish régime.' So far the argument of the Report was a plea for partitioning Posnania in accordance with nationality and without regard to historic frontiers. But having established the principle, its authors set out to justify a division which, in their own words, resulted in an 'obvious disproportion'—'the Polish majority received the smaller, and the German minority the larger part of the province'. 'The demarcation, though not easy, could have been drawn in accordance with the prevailing nationality—but a much more difficult problem arises over the fortress of Poznań. . . . Even if no Germans lived in Poznań, hardly a German would, under present conditions, allow that fortress to pass into other hands.' In declaring to have thus 'proved the necessity' of retaining it, they added that the fortress required a territorial belt—a glacis —and a safe connexion with the hinterland. Other arguments followed, sentimental, economic, or cultural. But then the question arose how districts with a Polish population could be represented in the German National Assembly. Reply: 'Far more than two million Poles in Prussia[1] and Silesia' are already comprised.[2] The Report concludes with draft resolutions which admit the twelve members from Posnania to the Assembly; recognize provisionally General von Pfuel's line of 4 June, while reserving to the National Assembly the final settlement of the demarcation line; demand from Prussia national safeguards for the Germans in Polish Posnania; but declare that for the Poles in West Prussia their national (*volkstümlich*) development 'in

[1] East and West Prussia taken together.
[2] The figure of 'far more than two million Poles' in those provinces seems an exaggeration as the total population of East and West Prussia and Upper Silesia was in 1849 only about 3½ millions.

Church, education, literature, local administration and the law courts, and equal rights for their language within its territory' are already safeguarded by the vote on minorities passed by the National Assembly on 31 May.

The debate which ensued presents a curious contrast with the early days of the Revolution. In March the prospect of war with Russia worked in favour of the Poles; now its possibility supplied the chief argument for despoiling them ('among the wars which await us, that with Russia . . . is . . . most likely', and therefore Poznań must be retained). In March the demand of the Posnanian Germans for separation from the Grand-Duchy was based on the principle of national 'self-determination' (the term was already used, and misused, in 1848); now that a demarcation line flagrantly violating it had been drawn, Kerst, perhaps their foremost representative, described the alleged right of peoples 'to divide in accordance with nationality', as 'new-fangled', 'nowhere recognised', dangerous, and unrealizable in borderlands with a mixed population (moreover: 'in politics the *status possidendi* is decisive', and 'self-preservation is the First Commandment of the political catechism'). Then the Poles were extolled as the vanguard of revolution; now Prince Lichnowsky explained that sympathies for Poland were waning because wherever a revolution broke out, one could safely assume that Polish *émigrés* were at work. Then the dismemberment of Poland was a 'shameful wrong', and her restoration a 'sacred duty' of democracy; now it was discovered that the Partitions had overthrown 'an aristocracy which prevented the mass of the serfs from becoming a people', and that a tender concern for the fate of the Polish peasant (or even of the gentry— *vide* 1846) enjoined caution ('they are not ripe for restoration', argued Giskra, a Moravian German, of the Left Centre; 'and even were they ripe, there is a limit to our sympathies as also to our sense of justice'—'I stand by the Fatherland, by our Germany, and that is to me *über alles*'). To this he added a specifically Austrian argument: 'We have Slavs in Bohemia, Moravia, Styria, and Illyria. How will it affect their doings if over a Slav problem we show weakness, half-hearted hesitations, and pusillanimity?' The *rapporteur* of the Foreign Affairs Committee, Stenzel, concluded a speech full of tiresome historical erudition[1] with a similar appeal on behalf of the Polish

---

[1] The Frankfort Parliament was a highly academic assembly—it contained 49 University Professors and Lecturers, and 57 schoolmasters, and at least

peasants, whom Wilhelm Jordan, a member of the Left, described as 'not Polish but Prussian' in feelings.

Robert Blum sadly reflected on 'the inordinate taste for conquest (*Eroberungslust*) shown by our young and uncertain freedom', and asked why Posnania was to be partitioned, but Slesvig, Bohemia, and the Tyrol, claimed by Germany, were indivisible? (Curiously not even he ever chose, or ventured, to name West Prussia as a province of mixed nationality.) Schuselka, thinking of Austria, and trying to ward off the proposed partition of Posnania, vindicated the *Territorialpolitik* hitherto pursued by the National Assembly—'this must be our basis, for a great nation requires space (*Raum*) to fulfil its world destiny (*Weltberuf*) and I would rather die a thousand times than, for instance, renounce Trieste because they speak Italian'. (How far was Frankfort from the *Lebensraum*?) But he appealed to the German intellectuals—poets, historians, politicians—who in their writings had stigmatized the dismemberment of Poland, not to sanction a new partition, and reminded them of the promise of restoration pronounced by the Pre-Parliament and reaffirmed by the Fifty. Similarly Wiesner, another Austrian: 'What a contrast between then and now! Only a few months separate us from that great day, and we hasten to abrogate its verdict!' Count von Wartensleben, a *Junker* and not an intellectual, gave a frank account of the change of heart which he, in common with so many others, had undergone: he confessed his previous *Unklugheit* (lack of wisdom)—when he heard the King announce national reorganization for the Poles, he had said to his friends that 'the time had come for Prussia to proclaim the independence of Poland, and virtually to declare war on Russia'. Now he favoured the proposed partition of Posnania, advised the Poles to be satisfied with the bird in the hand, and to work on the basis offered to them. And Göden, from Posnania, once more echoed the old cry: 'Do justice to your ill-treated German brethren before you do it to a foreign nation!'

three-fourths of its members had been to a University (see Valentin, op. cit., vol. ii, p. 12). The presence of a great many historians and jurists set a mark on its debates, and in that on Posnania one speaker after another went over the historical background, till the audience wearied of it: which may have been one reason for the impatience shown when Venedey, near the end of the debate, supplied a remarkably well-informed and documented account of the Posnanian transactions since the outbreak of the revolution. Even now that speech is worth reading as perhaps the shortest, clearest, and most impartial account of those transactions.

There was hardly a speech devoid of significance, but the three outstanding performances in that debate, which was 'one of the landmarks and turning points in the history of the National Assembly',[1] were the speeches of Wilhelm Jordan, a Berlin Democrat of East-Prussian extraction, Janiszewski, the only Pole in the Frankfort Parliament, who had entered it with a watching brief for his people, and Ruge, a leader of the extreme Left. Jordan's was a clarion call of German nationalism, sounded from the benches of the Left: cold, cynical, and intense, it proclaimed principles on which Bismarck acted and in which German intellectuals revel, but which other nations, with a few exceptions, would hesitate to proclaim. He started by thus defining the issue: 'Are half a million Germans to live under a German Government and administration and form part of the great German Fatherland, or are they to be relegated to the inferior position of naturalised foreigners subject to another nation of lesser cultural content than themselves?' Whoever would vote for the latter would be 'at least unconsciously a traitor to his own people' (ein Volksverräter). He criticized those who preached a campaign against Russia, and remarked that anyhow the German nation of 45 millions required no Polish 'bulwark'. 'To wish for a restoration of Poland because her downfall fills us with just regret, I call imbecile sentimentality.' It was necessary 'to awaken a healthy national egotism without which no people can grow into a nation'. 'Our right is that of the stronger, the right of conquest'; '. . . legal rules nowhere appear more miserable than where they presume to determine the fate of nations. To employ them for fixing the course of nations is to spread out spider-webs as nets for eagles.' 'The preponderance of the German race over most Slav races, possibly with the sole exception of the Russians, is a fact . . . and against history and nature decrees of political justice are of no avail.' 'Mere existence does not entitle a people to political independence: only the force to assert itself as a State among the others.' And he concluded his speech with the cry: 'Freedom for all, but the power of the Fatherland and its weal above all!'[2]

The same night, in the Club of the Left, Blum moved the exclusion of Jordan but failed to carry it; still, a short time later, Jordan withdrew from the Club, and formed with some friends,

---

[1] Valentin, op. cit., vol. ii, p. 125.
[2] *Freiheit für alle, aber des Vaterlands Kraft und Wohlfahrt über alles!*

including Kerst and Viebig[1] (Poznań), a new group between the Left and the Right Centre.[2]

Janiszewski answered calumnies and misrepresentations in a dignified speech, solemnly prophetic in some of its utterances. Princes have destroyed the Polish State and partitioned Poland, but at least 'they did not declare a Polish province to be German'. 'Culture which withholds freedom . . . is more hateful and despicable than barbarism.' The forced incorporation of Poles in Germany will merely create for her so many enemies within. 'The Poles have been swallowed up, but, by God, it will not be possible to digest them.'[3]

If Jordan's speech was the reveille of German nationalism, Ruge's was the funeral oration of German revolutionary idealism. What recently was called 'a shameful wrong' is now being explained as 'a historic necessity'. What 'we want is freedom, the freedom of the people, because the people . . . has become capable of governing itself'. He eulogized the Poles as 'apostles of freedom'; they 'must not be expunged from history'. The Pre-Parliament and the Committee of Fifty, 'our revolutionary fore-runners', have pledged the honour of the German nation to the liberation of the Poles. 'We must not disavow our fathers; we must redeem their pledge. . . . Germany's honour demands . . . that she should put an end to the long oppression of the Slav peoples; . . . that we cease to be oppressors, and become the friends of liberated nations. . . . If we deal with our honour as solemn pledges and constitutional promises have been dealt with in the past, we shall perish as a nation, perish morally. . . .' 'Much has been said about historic rights. Here . . . the true historic right is in question, the right created by history, by the greatest event in history. . . . For never has a revolution encompassed the globe as great as that of 1848. It is the most humane in its principles, in its decrees and proclamations. . . . Men who do not comprehend its principles and cannot respond

[1] His daughter, Clara Viebig, a well-known German novelist, published in 1907 a most successful novel about Posnania, *Das schlafende Heer*, written in the anti-Polish spirit of her father.

[2] See Valentin, op. cit., vol. ii, p. 126.

[3] In one passage Janiszewski contradicted rumours that a separation of Posnania from Prussia had ever been intended: for this would have delivered both Poles and Germans into the hands of Russia; similarly Schuselka avowed that it was impossible even to start the work of restoring Poland from the German end. The Poles and pro-Poles had undergone a sobering experience since the days when the immediate manumission of Poland was demanded, and Janiszewski's contention was interesting but hardly accurate.

to the call of freedom, must not commit treason against the historic right of the Revolution of 1848.'

In his speech Ruge came very near foretelling *la trahison des clercs*. The years 1866 and 1870 turned him into a fervent admirer of Bismarck, and in 1877 he was highly flattered to accept from Bismarck an *Ehrensold* (honorary pension) of £50 a year.

In the divisions at the conclusion of the debate Blum's delaying motion for a Commission of Inquiry to proceed to Posnania, and for a new report, was rejected by 333 against 139 votes, with 85 registered as absent and one abstention. After that the resolutions of the Committee, confirming the partition of Posnania and admitting its representatives to full membership in the Assembly, were carried by 342 votes against 31, with another 31 registered as abstaining, and 157 as absent—69 of those who had voted for Blum's motion declared that their demand for a further inquiry having been rejected, their conscience did not permit them to vote on data which they considered insufficient. As a last resort, or challenge, the pro-Poles reintroduced the resolution adopted in March and April, about the 'shameful wrong' and the 'sacred duty';[1] it was rejected by 331 votes to 101, with 26 registered as abstaining and 117 as absent. Of the 'Noes' 194, 'in order to prevent wrong use being made of their vote', explained their reasons, 'not for their own sake, but for that of the National Assembly, and for its justification before the world': 'that it is not incumbent on the Constituent Assembly to pronounce judgment on historic events, or to give indefinite promises for the future.' To which Moritz Hartmann (a Bohemian Jew and a popular writer of humorous verse)[2] added his own declaration: that he considered it unworthy by means of declarations to keep back-doors open for himself.

In the Prussian National Assembly the Radicals were stronger than at Frankfort; the Poles had sent representatives to Berlin, as the Diet bore a Prussian territorial, and not German national, character; both the Prussian Conservatives and the Roman Catholics, for obvious reasons of their own, were opposed to a partition of Posnania; and most good Prussians disliked central interference in Prussian affairs. On 30 August the Prussian Diet asked that the Frankfort Parliament should postpone fixing the final demarcation line in Posnania till the Prussian Diet had concluded their own inquiry into the matter (with which request

---

[1] See above, pp. 71 and 80.

[2] Of his best-known Hudibrastic production, *Die Reimchronik des Pfaffen Maurizius,* the first three instalments sold in about 30,000 copies.

the Prussian Government concurred); and on 29 October they voted by a majority of one, that within the framework of the Prussian State an undivided Posnania should be secured the rights promised in 1815. This resolution offended against the rule that federal decrees override those of State Legislatures, and against the two paragraphs of the German Constitution, voted on 19 October, that where non-German territories were joined under one ruler with territories of the German Confederation, their relations shall be based on 'personal union'. On 29 October the Frankfort Assembly therefore declared the resolution of the Prussian Diet void, and sent a Hessian general, von Schaeffer-Bernstein, to fix the demarcation line. He laid down the principle that no territory, once included in the German Confederation, could be separated from it, and consequently changes could only be made to the disadvantage of the Poles; and he finished by drawing a line which was geographically impossible, and which gave territory with 1,041,800 inhabitants to Germany, and with 308,900 to the Poles.[1] This was the verdict not of Prussian *Junkers*, but of the German National Assembly of 1848.

In 1849 the scheme of partitioning Posnania was dropped, without a special status for the province or 'minority rights' for the Poles being secured in the new Prussian Constitution.

XVIII

Both the Austrians who had sat in the Pre-Parliament were included in the Committee of Fifty: but to establish its claim to authority, a stronger representation was required for a State to which 190 seats were assigned in the National Assembly. It was therefore decided to co-opt six more Austrians: among them Francis Palacký, the foremost leader of the Czech national movement. In a letter, dated Prague, 11 April, he declined the invitation:[2]

The declared aim of your Assembly is to put a Federation of the German People (*Volksbund*) in the place hitherto held by the Federation of Princes (*Fürstenbund*), to make the German nation attain real unity, to strengthen its national feeling, and to enhance Germany's power at home and abroad. . . . I am not a German. . . .

I am a Bohemian of Slav race. . . . The rulers of our people have for centuries participated in the Federation of German Princes but the people never looked upon itself as part of the German nation. . . .

[1] These figures yield yet another sum total for the population of Posnania.   [2] See Palacký, *Gedenkblätter* (1874), pp. 149–55.

When I direct my gaze beyond the frontiers of Bohemia . . . I turn it not towards Frankfort but towards Vienna. . . .

. . . Indeed, if the Austrian Empire did not exist, in the interest of Europe, nay, of humanity, it would be necessary to make haste and create it.

Thus, to escape the German clutches, the Czechs seized the hand of their old enemies, the Habsburgs, and proceeded to develop the programme and ideology of *Austro-Slavismus*—of an Austria reconstructed on a predominantly Slav basis.

Within the Habsburg Monarchy there was parallelism, or even convergence, between the national programmes of the four master-races, the Germans, Magyars, Italians, and Poles. Had western Austria been torn from its setting and fitted into a Greater Germany, Vienna's Imperial claims on Hungary would have lapsed, Lombardy and Venetia could have gone their own way, and so could the Poles (had there been anywhere for them to go). And vice versa: had the Magyars and Italians succeeded in breaking away, this would have released the German, or partly Germanized, core of Austria, the original Habsburg *Erbländer* (hereditary possessions), and enabled the Austrian Germans to effect their complete union with Germany—*den innigen Anschluss an Deutschland*. But while the territorial claims of the four master-nations were, on the whole, non-competing,[1] they cut across the lands of the subject races, separating the Czechs from the Slovaks, the Slovenes from the Croats and Serbs, and the Ruthenes of Carpatho-Russia and Rumans of Transylvania from those of Galicia and the Bukovina; and these fragments were to be fitted into States with a sharply marked national character: the Czechs and Slovenes were to be forced into a Greater Germany; the Slovaks, Croats and Serbs, most of the Rumans, and one branch of the Ruthenes, into a Magyar State; and the rest into a new Poland—if such arose.

A resurrection of Poland presupposed a crushing defeat of Russia. The 'four-nation pattern' was essentially anti-Russian,

---

[1] No claims to the Burgenland (detached from Hungary in 1919) were raised by the Austrian Germans in 1848. Claims to Teschen were urged by the Poles against the Czechs, but not against the German Confederation; nor did they raise against the Magyars claims carried in 1919 and 1938 against the Slovaks—the community of the master-races seems to have had a marvellously soothing influence. Nor did the Italians raise against Hungary the claim to Fiume which they enforced against Yugoslavia in 1919. In 1848 the only serious clash between the four master-nations within the Habsburg Monarchy was that of the Germans and Italians over the Trentino and Trieste.

but this hostility was felt or exhibited in varying degrees. The Poles, openly and consistently, preached an anti-Russian crusade: hostility to Russia was the guiding principle and touchstone of their political activities. The Germans started on an anti-Russian line, but those of the Reich were soon deflected from it, largely by the conflict in Posnania; while the Austrian Germans, who had no quarrel with the Poles but with the Czechs and Slovenes, continued to fear and hate Russia as the champion of the smaller Slav nations and of Greek Orthodoxy. Still more so did the Magyars, who, however, at first prudently tried, but finally failed, to avoid a collision with Russia. Inversely, neither from the angle of power politics nor of the monarchical interest, could the Tsarist Government have viewed with indifference the rise of a Greater Germany, one and indivisible, and based on popular sovereignty. Further, the claim to a protectorate over Greek-Orthodox populations, Slav or non-Slav, was one of the oldest traditions of Moscow, which even St. Petersburg could not discard: it had been pressed against Poland, it was asserted in Turkey, and even the reactionary interest which Russia shared with the Habsburgs could not make her disinterest herself completely in their Serb, Ruman, and Little Russian (or Ruthene)[1] subjects. Her attitude towards the Roman-Catholic Czechs and Slovenes, Slovaks and Croats, was less clear; the consciousness of a Slav community, transcending religious divisions, was rising, but as yet did not influence official Russian policy, and was naturally frowned upon by the numerous highly placed Germans, Baltic and immigrant.[2] But Tsar, Government, and the Russian nation were at one in their hostility to the Poles, especially while these claimed—as they did, invariably and emphatically—dominion over 'Ruthene'[3] lands. To Nicholas I the Polish question was as

[1] Most of these were Uniats, but there was at all times a movement among them for a return to the Greek Orthodox Church, severely repressed by the Austrian Government, especially because of its obvious political connotation. Later on, when an anti-Russian Ukranian movement arose in East Galicia, the Uniat Church assumed a new political significance, differentiating its followers both from the Roman Catholic Poles and from Greek Orthodox Russia.

[2] On 7 July Meyendorff, whose son was taking a letter from the Tsar to Windischgrätz, wrote to Nesselrode: 'I am glad he will see at close quarters Pan-Slavism and its fruits. . . . It is the most horrible (*affreuse*) and the stupidest of the revolutionary products of our time' (*Briefwechsel*, vol. i, pp. 108-9).

[3] The Polish attempts to break up the unity of Russia's territory, nationality, and Church, have in turn brought forth Russian attempts at destroying Poland's political, and even cultural, existence. Russia's

much the touchstone of his politics as hostility to Russia was of theirs. When in March 1848 Count Thun, Austrian Minister in Stockholm, came on a special mission to St. Petersburg, the Tsar inquired whether Austria proposed to grant separate constitutions to her Italian provinces, Hungary, and Galicia. He spoke in cordial terms about Austria, but declared:[1]

> I could not tolerate a centre (un foyer) of insurrection at my door, and in touch with my friends, the Poles; if such a change was intended, or if a revolution broke out in Galicia, and was not vigorously put down, I should be forced, against my will, to intervene, and I would not hesitate one moment to cross the Austrian frontier and re-establish order in the name of the Emperor Ferdinand.

But the fears of an anti-Russian coalition, which were entertained in the early days of the revolution,[2] were soon allayed; Russia withdrew into the background, and the others, while spinning their schemes, paid curiously little attention to her: till she emerged in the summer of 1849, to quell the Hungarian revolution (in which a few thousand Poles were fighting), and in November 1850, at Olmütz to put an end to Prussian schemes of German unity, though these were monarchical in character.

Meantime two rival patterns were shaping within the Habsburg Monarchy: the master-races and the subject nationalities were becoming increasingly conscious of the community and conflict of interests which welded them into two groups. Evi-

crimes against Poland are more spectacular and better known, and have earned Poland much sympathy, while the other side of this age-long struggle has received little attention. Lord Salisbury was one of the few European statesmen, or even writers, who were aware that there was that other side to the Polish-Russian conflict—see his essay on "Poland" published in the *Quarterly Review* in Apr. 1863, and republished in his *Essays*, volume on *Foreign Politics* (1905), pp. 3–60.

[1] See Guichen, *Les Grandes Questions Européennes*, vol. i, p. 79.

[2] In the beginning of March it was widely believed in Russian Government circles that an extension of the revolution to Austria and northern Germany might result in an anti-Russian crusade such as the Poles hoped and worked for. Thus Meyendorff wrote to Nesselrode on 8 Mar. (op. cit., vol. i, p. 42):

> Then will come for us the decisive moment—the struggle with a Poland supported by all Europe, by France, Germany, Hungary, etc. With God's help we shall pull through like in 1812, but this is a terrible kind of war which has cost us dear, and in which it might be necessary to move the masses—who knows?—perhaps with *promises*, in order to tear them from the hands of our enemies.

What he presumably was thinking of was the possible need of raising a revolt of Russian peasants against their Polish landlords—a rather hazardous idea in a Baltic Baron.

dence of this consciousness among the master-races is met at every turn; here only a few illustrations shall be adduced. On 14 May the Hungarian Government sent two leading Magyar deputies to Frankfort to salute the German National Assembly, and establish co-operation; their commission was read in the Assembly on 24 May amid universal applause. On 1 July the question of the alliance which the Magyars had come to negotiate, was raised by Hartmann:

> Their wish, which certainly is also ours, could not be realised so long as we had no Executive. I move that now . . . the matter should be put on its agenda. Whoever bears in mind that the Hungarians are for a second time called upon to act as vanguard against barbarism, and that they are wedged between the Slavs, will understand the reasons behind my motion.

It passed unopposed. In the Hungarian Parliament, on 3 August, the demand for a close German-Magyar alliance was voted unanimously. In the debate Magyar antagonism to Austria's continued existence, and the desire to see her western provinces firmly embedded in a united Germany (so as to lay the ghost of the *Gesammtmonarchie*) found emphatic expression.[1]

> Whoever opposes the union of the *Erbländer* with Germany [declared Count Ladislas Teleki] commits treason against Germany, and treason against Austria. There is no such thing as Austrian patriotism. It is about as unthinkable as a specific patriotism on the various estates of Prince Esterhazy. Hitherto Austria was not a State but a family seized of divers possessions. . . . Where so far no bond existed between the *Erbländer*, it shall now be provided by fusion into the German Reich.

Kossuth, though a Minister of the Crown, descanted on 'the party of reaction and the Slav element' having gained the upper hand in Vienna, and concluded: 'Austria can only be saved by the closest possible union of the *Erbländer* with the German Federal State, which in turn will enter into a firm alliance with a free Hungary.' With regard to Italy, he, who as Minister of Finance, had to move the army vote, clearly hinted on 20 July that a victory of Austria was not in the Magyar interest; while Opposition speakers declared in so many words that by supporting Austria in Italy the Magyars would be undermining their own political existence, for having finished with the Italians, the dynasty would gather its forces and turn them against Hungary[2] (which, in fact, it did). Lastly, in order to detach the Poles from the other Austrian Slavs, and to establish a decisive German

---

[1] See Springer, op. cit., vol. ii, p. 480.   [2] Ibid., pp. 474-8.

superiority over the Czechs and Slovenes, the Magyars favoured independent status for Galicia, with complete Polish dominion over the Ruthenes. Still, while engaged in a mortal struggle against the Croats and Serbs, the Hungarian Government had to compromise with Vienna, and try to avoid giving offence to Russia. They therefore declared themselves ready 'to defend Austrian interests in Italy provided the Austrian Government offered its good services for the reduction of Croatia, and, at the end of the war, conceded all justified national demands of the Italians';[1] and inquiries about Russian troop concentrations on the Hungarian frontier having elicited the reply that 'Russia would undertake no action against Hungary so long as no movements hostile to her occurred in Hungary', a certain reserve was at first exercised towards the Poles.[2]

The Poles in the Vienna Parliament were divided into three groups. The Polish peasants,[3] moved by dislike and distrust of the Polish gentry, followed the late Governor of Galicia, Count Franz Stadion (returned by an East-Galician rural constituency) and the Ruthene priest Shashkevich, and sat on the Right, with the Slav *bloc* comprising the Ruthenes, Czechs, and most of the Slovenes. Nine Conservative Poles, among them four of the biggest aristocrats (Prince J. Lubomirski, and Counts Tytus Dzieduszycki, Adam Potocki, and Z. Zamoyski) and Bishop Wierzchlejski,[4] sat in the Centre. Averse to revolution, they had the sense to perceive that it was not likely to succeed, and that even if it did, German and Italian unity and Magyar

---

[1] See Springer, op cit., vol. ii, p. 475.   [2] Ibid., p. 472.

[3] I have so far failed to ascertain the number of Polish peasants in the Austrian Parliament of 1848. Jointly with the Ruthene peasants, it is usually given as 38, but it is not certain that this figure does not include one or two Ruthenes from the Bukovina, a small province which, at that time, was administratively joined to Galicia, and of which one part is Ruthene. It might perhaps be possible to ascertain the facts from the *Verhandlungen des österreichischen Reichstages, 1848–49*, but these are not in the British Museum.—Count L. Dunin-Borkowski, himself a member, alleges that eight Polish peasants, named by him, went with the gentry; see *Sejm ustawodawczy rakuzki* (1849), p. 24 (*The Austrian Legislative Assembly*)—there is a German translation of the first part of the book. Further evidence would be required before accepting Borkowski's statement. Smolka, writing to his wife on 19 Aug. 1848, utters the *cri de cœur*: 'If only in the impending by-elections members of the intelligentsia were returned' (op. cit., p. 17).

[4] The other four were: two big landowners, E. Kraiński and J. Jaruntowski, a barrister, Dylewski, and Father Bilecki (see Ziemiałkowski, op. cit., vol. i, p. 12). They were subsequently joined by Father Kozakiewicz; but as in the meantime Potocki had resigned his seat, their number remained the same.

independence might, by creating a void round Galicia, deliver it into the hands of Russia: hence they saw a Polish interest in the survival of the Habsburg Monarchy, and favoured Austro-Slavism. But the main body of the Polish members, including 40 out of 49 Poles *en redingote*,[1] typical 'liberals' or revolutionaries of 1848, sat on the Left, with the German Radical Nationalists. The programme of this Polish 'National Party' is contained in a paper drawn up by their most eminent leader, F. Smolka, apparently in October 1848, when he was offered a place in the Austrian Cabinet[2]—it is a full and unreserved *exposé* of the 'four-nation scheme', in which the rights of the subject races receive no consideration:

Seeing that Austria herself has proclaimed the idea of equal rights for her nationalities with a view to putting down the revolution, and has played off the Serbs, Croats, and Rumans against the Magyars, the Czechs against the Germans, and the Ruthenes against the Poles; seeing further that the idea must daily gain in strength—the further preservation of Austria in her present composition has become downright impossible. A complete constitutional reconstruction must therefore be attempted.

While sincerely conceding citizen rights and freedoms, Austria should revert to her old historic basis and accept the Crown of the German-Roman Empire which the Germans press on her, and unite *Germany* in one Empire.

Austria should renounce her *Italian* provinces and return them to the Italian nation which desires to be united.

To the Hungarians Austria should restore their constitution with a view to their establishing a Realm of the Lower Danube (*Unteres Donaureich*) with which Austria would remain connected by *personal union*.

Galicia should be given a completely separate government and national institutions with the declared purpose that it should form the nucleus (the crystallizing point) of the future Poland. Galicia is similarly to be connected with Austria by the bond of personal union.

Thus Austria can succeed in becoming a solid German State with such beautiful annexes as Poland and Hungary, and the territories dependent on them.

[1] *Polen im Frack*—so-called in contradistinction to the peasants. Ostaszewski-Barański states (op. cit., pp. 263–5) that the 100 Galician members included, besides 38 peasants and Stadion, 44 big landowners and intelligentsia, 15 priests, and two Jews. Of the priests, five were Poles. But his list of Poles other than peasants contains only 48 (instead of 49) names, as he has omitted Count Potocki.

[2] See K. Widmann, *Franciszek Smolka* (1884), pp. 414–15 (there is a German translation of the book). The author seems to have had the paper from Smolka himself; its precise date is not given.

When in August 1848 the Austrian Court and military, having vanquished the Italians, turned against Hungary, the German and Polish nationalists openly showed pro-Magyar sympathies; and when on 19 September a deputation from the Hungarian Parliament, which was moving fast towards a break with the Habsburgs, asked to be heard by the Vienna Parliament, the Left voted for receiving them.[1] The October Revolution in Vienna broke out over an attempt to prevent German regiments from marching against Hungary: it was obvious that a centralized, dynastic *Gross-Oesterreich* would put an end to dreams of German unity no less than to those of Italian or Hungarian independence. And the rump Parliament which remained in Vienna during the revolution, consisted almost entirely of Germans and Poles,[2] and was presided over by Smolka. On one occasion, however, this Polish leader had annoyed the Germans: when on 21 August, after Radetzky's victory over the Italians, he argued in favour of a solution of the Italian question 'which would make the Italians into friendly neighbours'. For even in German nationalists the Italian problem was apt to reawaken an Austrian patriotism—an old mutual dislike and the conflict over the Trentino and Trieste divided them from the Italians. On 13 June 1848, in the Vienna Committee of Public Safety (*Sicherheitsausschuss*), probably the most Radical organization in Austria, Adolf Fischhof, its chairman, declared that they would not have wished to fight a people who wanted to be free, but now 'the honour of the Austrian arms' (*Oesterreich's Waffenehre*) was at stake: 'in 1809 and 1813 we were patriots though bond, we shall be it now when free.'[3]

Divided and competing loyalties in the Austrian Germans were the main factor which disturbed the harmony of the 'four-nation pattern' within the Habsburg Monarchy. In every

---

[1] The motion was rejected by 186 to 108 votes; 36 Poles voted with the minority, and 12 with the majority—five peasants, and at least four Conservatives (Lubomirski, Dzieduszycki, Zamoyski, and Kraiński; Potocki was absent, but subsequently declared his agreement with them); not one Polish peasant voted for the Magyars (see Smolka, op. cit., pp. 49–50). Three Slovenes voted for admitting the Magyars; see Geist-Lanyi, *Das Nationalitätenproblem auf dem Reichstag zu Kremsier, 1848–1849* (1920), p. 101.

[2] There remained also two Czechs, Father Sidon and a pensioned official, Sadil (see Geist-Lanyi, op. cit., p. 57), and several Slovenes (ibid., p. 68). In the Frankfort Parliament an Austrian German, von Mayfeld, having described the Vienna Revolution as 'distinctly German, distinctly anti-Slav', denounced the Czechs as 'oblivious of their duty and honour when they left Vienna'!   [3] See R. Charmatz, *Adolf Fischhof*, p. 52.

Austrian German there was an Austrian and a German, and comparatively few had made their choice or were prepared either to renounce union with Germany in order to preserve the Austrian Empire, or to sacrifice Austria for the sake of a Greater Germany: most of them vaguely hoped, and made fumbling attempts, to be an integral part of both, flaunting their *Deutschtum* in Vienna, the capital of an Empire of whose population only one-fifth was German.[1] 'The German National Assembly cannot have a better right to build up Germany than the Austrian to preserve Austria', wrote one of the leading Austrian members in the Frankfort Parliament.[2] 'The Austrian Germans . . . will be Germans', declared another, 'so long as you do not unreasonably exact from them (*ihnen zumuthen*) that they cease being Austrians.'[3] They oscillated between *Gross-Oesterreich* and *Gross-Deutschland*, aspiring to continue in both a primacy to which they felt entitled as heirs, or at least co-partners, of the Habsburgs (another example of a 'democracy' assuming the legacy of a dynasty or oligarchy).[4] They tried to exert within a united Germany an influence based on the weight of the Austrian Empire, and within that Empire to assert a superiority based on being a branch of the German nation. Here was a baffling, equivocal situation, overcome at times by affecting a deliberate over-emphasis of one aspect, but

---

[1] Anton Springer, who had not yet gone over completely to the German nationalists, wrote in 1850: 'If the existence of a united Austria was deemed a historic necessity, Vienna should have set the same limits to its national feelings which it wished to impose on the non-German nationalities, but if it could not withstand the call of nationalism, it should in fairness have respected it also in others' (*Oesterreich nach der Revolution*, p. 15).

[2] Sommaruga in *Oesterreichs Zukunft und dessen Stellung zu Deutschland*; it is not in the British Museum, and is quoted here after W. Schüssler, *Die nationale Politik der oesterreichischen Abgeordneten im Frankfurter Parlament* (1913), p. 27.

[3] Beidtel, member for Brno (in Moravia), speaking in the Frankfort National Assembly on 24 Oct. 1848. As pamphleteer he often used the anagram of Tebeldi.

[4] The programme of *Mittel-Europa* (like most ideas in European history during the last hundred years) can, in fact, be discerned in 1848. Perthaler, an Austrian member of the Frankfort Parliament, argued in his pamphlet, *Das Erbkaisertum Klein-Deutschland* (quoted after Schüssler, op. cit., p. 30) that the outer line of the German polity must extend from France to Russia and that the small nationalities in that zone have no right to an independent existence, and can live only under German rule—'for this alone is tolerant and just'. 'The small nationalities may therefore partake of the blessings of the German polity, but must not go counter to it.' There is to be but one political system in Central Europe: 'because the Germans are the only powerful nation in Central Europe, that system must be German.'

never fully resolved in the emotions of the great mass of the Austrian Germans. The dream of *Mittel-Europa* in 1915–18 was an attempt at reconciling the two divergent aspirations of the German Austrians: and it proved the ruin of Bismarck's *Klein-Deutschland*.

XIX

The principle of equal rights for the Czech people and language was readily accepted by the Prague Germans in the early days of the Revolution. It proved less pleasing in its practical application: the aspect of the city was changing; in street inscriptions Czech was displacing German, the Czech national colours and dress were much in view, talking Czech in public was becoming *bon ton*. Equality failed to find its epitome in a tender scene of patronage thankfully received (with tears of gratitude on the one side, and of self-approbation on the other): these educated, or half-educated, Czech peasants and *petit bourgeois* were setting up on their own. The Students' League broke up, and a 'Slavia' ranged itself (as yet fraternally) by the side of a 'Teutonia'; the Czechs left the literary society 'Concordia', and formed the 'Svornost', &c. Innocuous intellectual activities of a 'folk-character', hitherto countenanced by the Germans, were assuming a political complexion. In the first petition carried from Prague to Vienna the emphasis was on equal rights for the two nations and the liberal decalogue of political freedoms; in the second, drawn up on 28 March and no longer supported by the Germans, it shifted to the claims of the 'Bohemian State-Right', the ancient rights of the Crown of St. Wenceslas: its lands were to be reunited, and to receive a very wide measure of home-rule—a common Diet for the Czech provinces of Bohemia, Moravia, and Austrian Silesia, and a Ministry responsible to it. On 8 April the Vienna Government virtually acceded to the Czech demand for a responsible government (*verantwortliche Central-behörden*) in Prague, but the question of a union of the three Czech provinces was reserved for the future Austrian Parliament (gentle ambiguities and reservations being all the Vienna Government were capable of in those days of ready assent to mutually contradictory programmes). Still it looked as if a provincial Constituent Assembly were to meet in Prague before an Austrian Parliament was convened in Vienna—which would have been a step towards a federalization of the Habsburg Monarchy, but on lines cutting across the 'four-nations scheme'. Although most of the Bohemian aristocrats spoke German at home (unless they preferred French), a good many favoured the Czech programme: in truly feudal territorial magnates, as in ruling dynasties, there is a *penchant* towards the people who inhabit their lands; moreover a preference for being princes in their own province rather than courtiers in the capital. Acid nationalisms based on language (on plenty of it and little in it) originate mainly with urban middle-class intellectuals: and this is why 1848 is of such supreme importance in the growth of European nationalisms.

The German reaction to the Czech national movement and programme started in the 'Sudeten' fringe and among the 'Sudetens'[1] resident in Vienna. The situation resembled that in Posnania: the Germans in Prague, as in Poznań, were at first inclined to be moderate and conciliatory; Reichenberg, Eger, Saatz, and Budweiss played the part of Bromberg, Czarnikau, and Meseritz. In Vienna an association of Germans 'from Bohemia, Moravia, and Silesia' was formed to oppose the national claims of the Czechs and to defend 'the national rights' of the Germans. About the time when the second Czech deputation returned from Vienna, the invitation to Frankfort had reached Palacký; the Czechs were summoning the 'Sudeten' Germans to the Constituent Diet in Prague, the Germans were summoning the Czechs to the National Assembly in Frankfort—and over this issue the main battle was joined. The Germans in Prague would have formed a numerically and culturally influential minority, and the connexion with Vienna, even if merely federal, would have added to their importance and security; the Czechs in Frankfort would have been *une quantité négligeable*, and their inclusion would have been a complete negation of their political existence: which, indeed, was denied by those who summoned them. They therefore turned their gaze to Vienna, and to the possibilities offered by an Austrian Parliament. Within the Habsburg Monarchy the Slavs, especially together with the Rumans (who shared the interests of the other subject-races in Hungary), had a decisive majority over the Germans and Magyars.[2] But could their policies be blended into common

---

[1] The description is both anachronistic and inaccurate, but convenient.

[2] Springer (a Czech by birth but a German by choice) gives the following percentages for the various races within the Habsburg Monarchy about 1850: German 23, Czechoslovak 19, Magyar 14, Italian, Ruthene, and Ruman 8 each, Polish 7, Serb 5, Slovene and Croat 4 each; see *Geschichte Oesterreichs*, vol. ii (1865), p. 4, n. 1. The figures of Germans and Magyars were undoubtedly padded with Yiddish-speaking Jews and with 'bi-lingual' Slavs: even so the Germans and Magyars together formed only 37 per cent. as against 47 per cent. Slavs (not counting the Rumans). But the four master-

action? Would the Poles co-operate? Their prestige in Europe and position in Austria were such that the Slav movement could hardly succeed without them, still less against them. By August 1848, the disposition of pieces on the European chess-board was made, and the problems were set: but in the spring policies were only beginning to take shape—there was groping and hesitation, dim, intuitive perceptions of the dominant interests intermingled with theoretical beliefs. It is the confused interplay of nascent ideas and of policies in the making, which imparts a singular interest to the Slav Congress of May–June 1848.

The Slav renaissance of the Romantic Period,[1] harking back to distant common origins, had prepared the ground for such a gathering. The western and southern Slavs, having lost their upper and middle classes in the catastrophes of the preceding three or four centuries, had changed into peasant nations. The advance of democracy and the Romantic movement (with its idealization of the past and of 'folk' elements) favoured a rebirth of obliterated nations from their roots; and as the Slav languages are close to each other,[2] and are linked still further by inter-mediary formations, the idea was current, especially among the 'a-historical' Slav peoples, that their different tongues were but dialects or variants of one common speech (a linguistic Slav 'Q'), and Slavdom one body; a comparison was drawn with the German *Stämme*—Saxons, Bavarians, Suabians, &c.—whose dialects differ as widely as the various Slav languages. But the missing tie of a common literary language caused the difference: and an attempt was made to replace this by a cultural 'Slav reciprocity' —a literary community and interchangeability transcending 'tribal' divisions. Even among the Poles, Latin Westerners by inclination and vanity, the Romantic period produced a de-flexion towards the distant, truly Slav past of their people.

When after the outbreak of the March Revolution delegations

nations taken together formed 52 per cent. of the population, possessed of a very marked social, economic, and cultural superiority.

[1] For a brilliant sketch of the Czech Renaissance, see E. Denis, *La Bohême depuis la Montagne-Blanche* (1903), vol. ii. A good study covering all Slav nations is Milan Prelog, *Slavenska Renesansa, 1780–1848* (1924); the book is in Croat.

[2] The name *Slav* is derived from *slovo*, which, in all Slav languages, means 'word'—they were the 'worded ones', who could understand each other, whereas the Germans, who merely mumbled (*mye-mye*), were the *myemtsy*, which changed into *Nyemtsy*, the name common for them with all Slavs; *nyemy* also means 'dumb'. The names of two of the Slav nations—the Slovaks and the Slovenes—are mere variants of the racial cognomen.

from Slav nationalities—Poles, Czechs, and Slovenes, Slovaks, Croats, and Serbs—arrived in Vienna with petitions to the Emperor and the Government, each pursued its own particular aims, and not one spoke of a common Slav cause—in 1848 the Slav movement, which had started with philologists, poets, writers, historians, and antiquaries, was only beginning to assume a political character. Still, casual meetings between the delegates seemed first to have suggested the idea of a Slav Congress.[1] It matured under pressure from the Germans and Magyars: Posnania was being partitioned, and more and more of it incorporated in the new Germany; the Czechs and Slovenes were summoned, with growing emphasis, to send members to the Frankfort Parliament, and thus to recognize its sovereign jurisdiction over their lands; the Magyars, with the feeble acquiescence of a distracted Vienna Government, were assuming sole authority over the Slovaks, Croats, and Serbs. Was it not time for the Slavs, numerous but divided, to draw together, to co-ordinate political activities, and create an effective counter-weight to the German National Assembly and the Hungarian Parliament? Towards the end of April the idea of a Slav Congress took shape, the initiative coming from three different quarters. Štur, a Slovak refugee from Magyar persecution, canvassed it in Prague Radical circles; Moraczewski broached it in the Posnania National Council, and with its consent transmitted the suggestion to Prague; and on 20 April Kukuljević put it forward in the leading Croat paper. His article, reprinted in Prague by K. Havliček[2] on 30 April, was read the same morning in a gathering of Czech literary men, who decided to act after having secured the support of Palacký and Šafařik, the two foremost Czech intellectuals,[3] and of Slavophil members of the Bohemian aristocracy.

It would be of the highest interest to trace, step by step, the story of the Slav Congress; there, as elsewhere, 1848 was a seed-plot of history. But this cannot be done here, both for reasons

[1] See Čejchan, 'Ke vzniku myšlenky slovanského sjezdu roku 1848' ('The Origin of the Idea of a Slav Congress in 1848'), in the Czech review *Slovanský Přehled*, vol. xx (1928), pp. 401–8. The Prague gathering of 1848 is known as the 'Slav'—not 'Pan-Slav'—Congress, which seems to reflect the conception of Slav unity.

[2] Havliček was perhaps the greatest journalist whom the Czechs have produced, and one of the makers of their national renaissance. A book about him, first published in 1904, is one of President Masaryk's outstanding works—but there is no copy of it in the British Museum.

[3] Šafařik was a Slovak by birth.

of space and because much even of the printed material is lacking in this country. I must therefore limit myself to a brief general survey.[1]

The preparatory work for the Congress devolved mainly on the Czechs. The initial question, who was to be invited, was of crucial importance: was it to be a Slav Congress, or a Congress of Austrian Slavs? An effective restriction of membership to Austrian subjects would have been a declaration in favour of the Habsburg Monarchy and of Austro-Slavism; it would have turned the Congress into a Slav Pre-Parliament for Vienna. This would have suited the outlook and served the purpose of the cautious, realistic Czech leaders: and as there were no Czechs or Slovaks anywhere outside the Austrian Empire, such a limitation would have entailed no national renunciation on their part. Even the Yugoslavs might have accepted it: the fate of those still under the Turks was not in question at that juncture. But the Poles, at the high tide of revolutionary hopes and dreams, could hardly be expected to endorse frontiers drawn in the Partitions, to plan their future within the framework of Austria, and by implication to renounce national reunion as the immediate goal of their political endeavours. Moreover, on their side the proposal of a Slav Congress originated in Posnania: threatened, like the Czechs, by the aggressive German nationalism focused in Frankfort, the Posnanians wished for a common front: whereas of all the Poles the Galician were perhaps least inclined to any form of 'Slavism'. Facing Russia on an exceed-

[1] There are contemporary accounts by members of the Congress (the Czech Vocel, the Poles Moraczewski and Malisz, the Lusatian Sorb J. P. Jordan, &c.) and numerous memoirs bearing on the subject. But for a long time little could be found in the way of minutes, either of the full Congress, or of its three Sections (Czechoslovak, Polish-Ruthene, and Yugoslav): the Congress having broken up in the midst of riots, most of the material was destroyed or was hidden from the Austrian police. It is only in our own time that enough has come to light to render possible a more detailed study of the proceedings. There are now four important studies written from four national angles: by the Czech, Z. Tobolka (1901); by the Ukrainian, I. Bryk (1920); by the Croat, M. Prelog, the most comprehensive of all—it fills about half his book *Slavenska Renesansa, 1780–1848* (1924) (for a useful summary of it see H. Wendel in *Die Gesellschaft*, vol. iii); and by the Pole, W. T. Wisłocki (1928), who reproduces in full the minutes of the Polish-Ruthene Section, long deemed lost but rediscovered by him. Of these four studies only Wisłocki's is in the British Museum (while Prelog's I was able to secure privately). Besides there are books on cognate subjects and numerous studies in periodicals, Slav and German, which are not available in this country. A new and comprehensive account of the Slav Congress of 1848, written against the background of the European revolution, is required.

ingly long border, they feared and hated her, without having direct contacts or the motives for compromise which subjection is apt to supply; in Galicia they were in conflict with the Ruthenes; they disliked the Czechs;[1] their attitude towards the Austrian Government was still coloured by 1846; they had no concern with Frankfort, and sympathized with the 'revolutionary' programme of the Austrian Germans, the Magyars, and the Italians. In a Congress restricted to Austrian subjects, the Galicians would have been the sole representatives of the Poles; and yet to invite the Posnanians would have meant to abandon the Austrian, internationally Conservative, basis of the Congress, and to enter the stream of European revolution.

Palacký and Šafařik were great *savants*, of outstanding merit in their services to the Czech revival, but timid politicians.[2] While preserving their personal independence and national dignity, they had done their work under the protecting wing of well-disposed noblemen; and how else could it have been done under the Metternich régime for a nation half-submerged by the Germans? Even in 1848 they thought it inadvisable for the Czechs, in their precarious position, to engage in revolutionary adventures —and that in company with Germans and Magyars, who under cover of 'liberalism' were pursuing aggressively nationalist poli-

---

[1] Among the Austrian officials in Galicia, there were a good many Czechs. The Slovak Štur said in the Czechoslovak Section of the Slav Congress: 'Austria is the quintessence of servility, espionage, and similar dirt. What has Austria made of you, Czechs? She sent you to Poland (Galicia) as tools of the most shameful régime' (see Prelog, op. cit., p. 263). Ziemiałkowski, in his *Memoirs* (part ii, p. 35) speaks of 'the loathing which every Pole feels for the Czech'. The Czechs reciprocated those feelings. Jachim, a Czech resident in Lvov, wrote about the Poles to Palacký on 16 May 1848: 'Your noble and sacred ideas of Slav reciprocity are not valued by these people, except in so far as they can be made to serve their own particular purposes. With them stands in the forefront an independent Poland within her previous frontiers, i.e. including the Ruthene people whom they oppressed and further wish to oppress. Therefore your sweet reciprocity cannot suit their taste, for it aims at a real equality between nations to which they pay lip service but which they hate in their hearts' (see Prelog., op. cit., p. 306, and 'Boemus', 'Der Tschechische Panslavismus im Jahre 1848', in *Oesterreich*, vol. i, p. 522). Even Havliček doubted the possibility of co-operation with the Poles: their pride and intolerance allows them to acknowledge none but France and Poland, nor 'to speak or think of anything but the integral restoration of Poland' (Prelog, p. 287).

[2] President Masaryk rightly criticizes Palacký who advocated the reconstruction of Austria on a Slav basis, but when, on 8 May, he was offered the Ministry of Education, refused for fear of the storm which his acceptance would produce among the Germans (see *Karel Havliček*, pp. 115–16).

cies. Šafařik approved of the idea of a Slav Congress, but insisted on membership being limited to Austrian Slavs (others might be invited as guests, by private letters), and on an unequivocal expression of loyalty to Austria in the public appeal. Count Matthew Thun, a leading Bohemian nobleman, was elected chairman of the Organizing Committee, and accepted, having been assured of their 'faithful attachment to the Imperial House'. The Manifesto, signed by Czech intellectuals, a number of Bohemian aristocrats, and also by representatives of other Slav nations, and dated 1 May,[1] described the depressed, disjointed condition of the Slavs, called on them to unite, as other nations were doing, and named the attempts to subordinate Austria to a united Germany, and to engulf Austro-Slav provinces in it, as a reason for summoning a Congress 'of all Slav nations of the Austrian Empire'.[2] 'Should other Slavs not inhabiting the Austrian Empire wish to honour the Congress with their presence, they will be cordially welcomed as guests.' The conveners could do no more: nor could they do less.

But Palacký, fearing unfavourable reactions in official and German circles, proposed on 5 May an explanatory Address to the non-Slav nations of Austria, declaring in the strongest terms fidelity to 'the constitutionally ruling House of Habsburg-Lorraine', and the determination 'to preserve by every possible means the integrity and sovereignty of the Austrian Empire', repudiating all separatist, Pan-Slav, or pro-Russian sentiments, or any intention to dominate the non-Slavs in Austria, but claiming full and equal rights for all its nationalities. Grzybowski, a Pole resident in Prague, strongly voiced in the Organizing Committee Polish opposition to such a declaration of loyalty; Count Matthew Thun replied that if such were the feelings of the Poles they had better stay away, and Palacký that he could take no part in the Congress unless it declared for Austria. The Address was

---

[1] Apparently it did not appear till 5 May; see Prelog, op. cit., p. 282. It was published in five languages—Czech, Polish, Serbo-Croat, Lusatian Sorb, and German (but not in Ruthene); and there are marked differences between the various texts, and also between the lists of signatures, fresh ones being added in different impressions. Among the Polish signatories, the most prominent were Prince J. Lubomirski, a sincere Slavophil educated at Prague University, more important socially than politically; and Dobrzański, a journalist, very active in the Lvov National Council.

[2] The Manifesto stated that the inclusion of 'all Austrian countries other than Hungary' was intended—a curious lapse: there was never any idea of including Galicia, the Bukovina, Dalmatia, or Eastern Istria, which were not in the German Confederation.

published over twenty signatures of Czechs only.[1] But fears lest the Poles upset the Czech programme, and the Congress itself, continued to disturb the Organizing Committee,[2] warned, moreover, by Count Leo Thun, the newly appointed Governor of Bohemia, an ultra-Conservative, who had served in Galicia. On 22 May Grzybowski, obviously prompted by the Czechs, issued a warning to his countrymen, calling upon them to send only reasonable and moderate men—'the legal way intended for the work of the Congress is for us the only way'; 'let us . . . keep within the limits of the feasible, and learn to look upon Austria as a friend, after she has been forced by the *Zeitgeist* completely to change her policy; not only the present, but even our ultimate aims have ceased to be contrary to her interests'. Some twenty years later, after Czech Austro-Slavism had collapsed, this view became the basis of the Galician-Polish policy, carried on in partnership with the Germans and Magyars.

The Manifesto summoning the Congress was an uneasy compromise between acceptance of the Austrian Empire, whose subjects alone were to attend as members, and the ethnic principle, all Slavs being invited as guests. Some on the Organizing Committee would have gone even further in making the Congress an Austrian Pre-Parliament: should not the Rumans be invited? And since they met *qua* Austrians, should not the Bohemian Germans be included? But if so, why not all Austrian Germans?[3] The view prevailed that full agreement and co-operation between the Slavs must be secured before anyone

[1] The signatories included 4 counts, 2 barons, and 1 knight; it was a pre-eminently Conservative group. Four days later, on 9 May, some 60 Poles gathered at Breslau, including the chief leaders from Posnania, Marquis A. Wielopolski from Russian Poland, Prince J. Lubomirski and a few Galician Conservatives, and they drafted an Address to the Poles calling on all 'regardless of frontiers and shades of language' to take an active part in the Slav Congress. There is a Polish and a Czech text, and the Czech is signed by Libelt, Lipski, and Counts Roger Raczyński and August Cieszkowski— all four from Posnania: they ignored the limitation of active membership of the Congress to Austrian subjects. The two drafts were found by Wisłocki among the papers of Prince Lubomirski; there is no evidence of their having been published.

[2] At one meeting at which no Pole was present, Brauner told an anecdote of how peasants in the district of Sącz in West Galicia, when asked whether they were Poles, replied: 'We are quiet folk.' 'Then are you Germans?' 'We are decent folk.'

[3] The Galician Poles, for different reasons, would have wished the Magyars to be invited, but that suggestion seems never to have been put to the Organizing Committee.

else was approached: but a considerable minority would have wished the Germans present as witnesses to the eminently innocuous character of the Congress.

The Organizing Committee suggested that the Congress should sit in three Sections, corresponding to the territorial and historical divisions: I. the Czechoslovak, II. the Polish-Ruthene, III. the Yugoslav Section,[1] each to elect sixteen representatives to the Central Committee and to have *liaison* officers with the other two Sections. The draft Agenda named the following problems for discussion: Was an Alliance between the Austrian Slavs desired and, if so, what form should it take? What constitutional changes did they postulate within the Austrian Empire? What could be done to strengthen the cultural ties between Austrian and non-Austrian Slavs? What should be the attitude of the Austrian Slavs to the Frankfort Parliament? Should the resolutions of the Congress be submitted to the Emperor? The commentary on these leading questions supplied the Czech programme for the Congress. The preamble surveys the European scene: autocracy has run its course, a greater share in government is due to the people, oppressed nationalities are re-arising. The Austrian Empire is in danger of collapse, and its dismembered parts must not become the prey of neighbours. Lombardy and Venetia have broken away, in Hungary an armed conflict between Magyars and Yugoslavs is imminent, and the Emperor has left Vienna.

If the Ministers enjoyed so little of His Majesty's confidence that he did not consult them before leaving, why should the Slav peoples confide in them? They are known to think on German lines and to be guided by the party which, besides being revolutionary, is strongly hostile to the Slavs.

[1] To begin with, the third Section was called 'Illyrian', but subsequently changed its name to Yugoslav. The division into three Sections obviated linguistic difficulties: Czech and Slovak, and Slovene and Serbo-Croat are mutually understood. The difference between Polish and Ruthene is greater, but all educated Galician Ruthenes understood Polish, and the Poles from East Galicia (of whom there were a good many) understood Ruthene. The story that German was used at the Congress is a hostile invention, and even Kuranda, though anti-Czech, denied it in a speech in the Frankfort Parliament, on 1 July. There were no Bulgars or Lusatian Sorbs at the Congress (J. P. Jordan was an *émigré* who could no longer count as representative). Official Russia took a completely negative attitude, and only two Russians attended the Congress: the famous revolutionary, Michael Bakunin, and Olimpiy Miloradov, priest of a settlement of Old Believers in the Bukovina (he was presumably an Austrian subject). These two joined the Polish-Ruthene Section.

The salvation of the Slavs is in union. The Austrian Empire should be rebuilt as a Federal State, with equal rights for all the nationalities (but apparently separate Parliaments in Vienna and Budapest were envisaged). An alliance with Germany is acceptable,

but we Slavs cannot admit that Austria's sovereignty should be infringed, or that either we, or any other part of the Empire, should be incorporated in a foreign State. Never shall we acknowledge the sovereignty of Germany over us. The Emperor and King Ferdinand is, and will remain, our sole ruler. . . . We therefore solemnly protest against any steps taken in Austria, with or without Government consent, to elect members to the Frankfort Parliament.

Thus the Czechs objected even to the *Anschluss* of the German parts of Austria, for this would have deprived the Habsburg Monarchy of its territorial coherence;[1] but the enforced exclusion of German Austria from the Reich could morally be justified only by an Austrian separatism among its Germans—one more reason for Czech statesmen to play in with the Habsburgs.

XX

The Congress opened on 2 June. Palacký was chosen President, Prince Lubomirski and the Yugoslav Stanko Vraz, Vice-Presidents. The membership fluctuated, and no lists are complete (e.g. the three Poles who were subsequently to attain the greatest distinction, Smolka, Ziemiałkowski, and Marquis Wielopolski, though present for part of the time, appear in none). Vocel, in his semi-official 'Historical Account of the Slav Congress', published in the *Czech Museum Journal*[2] for 1848, puts the number of members at 340 (237 Czechs and Slovaks, 61 Poles, Ruthenes and Russians, and 42 Yugoslavs), and then, in an Appendix, gives a list of only 318 names. According to Wisłocki, there were another 24 registered Polish members and some 40 guests. Altogether, there were at the Congress about 500 members and 500 guests. Few came from Slovakia (15–20) for fear of Magyar reprisals; but besides Štur, they included Hurban and Hodža (their grandsons were again to play a prominent part in the Czechoslovak Republic). The Yugoslavs were mainly from Croatia and the Voyvodina—but there were among them also a few non-Austrian subjects from Serbia. Of crucial importance was the composition of the Polish-Ruthene Section: and this was

[1] The objection reappears in 1918 and 1945, for through the *Anschluss* a Greater Germany would encircle Czechoslovakia.
[2] 'Historická zpráva o sjezdu slovenském' in *Časopis Českého Museum*, 1848.

prejudged in a sense contrary to the original scheme when the Organizing Committee (against warnings from Leo Thun) devised a method whereby each Section selected its own members. This left the Poles free to accept non-Austrian subjects: of the 61 in Section II who appear in Vocel's list, 44 were Austrian, 10 Prussian, and 7 Russian subjects; and the Posnanian leader, Libelt, a man of outstanding ability and character, was elected Chairman of the Section: a coach and six was thus driven through the rule restricting membership to Austrian subjects.

In the Congress register the Czechs entered their place of residence, others, as a rule, their country or nationality. But one would search in vain the official list for a 'Pole': in that printed by Vocel, 21 members of Section II appear as 'Masurs', 21 as 'Ruthenes', and the rest mainly under provincial designations: the name of 'Pole' was kept in reserve—an attempt, both naive and artful, to link it up with territory of 1772 and make it cover everybody within those frontiers; Ukrainians, White Russians, and Lithuanians were to be levelled down and rank on an even with sub-divisions of the Polish-speaking population based on dialects or provinces. Further, of 21 'Ruthenes' only 8 were authentic, while the rest belonged to the Polish or Polonized nobility; and some of them (for instance, Prince Lubomirski) appeared one day as Ruthenes and on another as Masurs. It was a disingenuous trick with a genuine historic background: the type *natione Polonus, gente Ruthenus* had existed in the gentry-Republic in which these men were as representative of the western provinces of White Russia and the Ukraine as Grattan's Parliament was of Ireland. But by 1848 O'Connells had arisen also in East Galicia, and demanded to be heard on behalf of its peasant people: one purpose of the Galician Poles in attending the Slav Congress[1] was to stifle the voice of the genuine Ruthenes,

---

[1] According to Ziemiałkowski the Lvov National Committee decided to take part in the Congress in order not to leave the field to the 'Święto-Jurcy' (the Ruthenes grouped round the Greek-Catholic Cathedral of St. Jury, i.e. St. George); see *Memoirs*, part ii, p. 232. A modern Polish historian, S. Kieniewicz (op. cit., p. 257) frankly admits that one of the tasks of the Poles at Prague was to 'smudge over the ticklish Ruthene problem' (the expression used is *zatuszować*, which corresponds to the German *vertuschen*). The instructions of the Lvov National Council to Dobrzański and his colleagues (published by Wisłocki) seem also otherwise disingenuous: they were to appear as individuals and in no way to commit the Council, but were to act as one body under its orders, report to it, keep strictly to the lines laid down in its two Memoranda for the Emperor, to 'mediate' between the Slavs and the Magyars, &c.

whose aim, in turn, was to oppose and expose the Poles. No
wonder then if a great deal of the time of Section II was taken
up by bitter wrangling between them, the rest being employed
by the Poles in discussing fine points of procedure, in forming
a secretariat, electing committees, &c. The stage of taking up
the agenda prepared by the Organizing Committee was never
reached.

The Yugoslavs carried on without settled procedure: they
were pressed for time. The Serbs, gathered round Rajačić,
Metropolitan of Karlovać, and the Croats under Jellačić, their
Banus (Governor), were still carrying on an argument against
the Magyars at the Imperial Court in Innsbruck, but at any
moment the dispute threatened to change into a ferocious conflict.[1] They now asked the Congress to address the Emperor
in support of their own delegations. The Czechs were willing;
the Slovaks, exposed to Magyar reprisals, were slightly more
cautious; but the Poles merely wished to 'mediate', and devised
ingenious counter-proposals. In the end not one of the Galician
Poles would go to plead against the Magyars (and no others
could approach the Austrian Emperor). 'Gentlemen', said
Libelt, 'we are in a false position. . . . We are tainted with indifference and insincerity . . . our hearts are not with the cause
for which we are assembled. I discern it in the speeches, looks,
in everything: we are not sincere.'[2] Finally, the question of
a Congress delegation in support of the Yugoslavs had to be
left over.

The Czechoslovak Section adhered to the programme of 27
May, but even they proved tepid in their Austro-Slavism. The
Czech youth responded to the revolutionary enthusiasms of
1848 more than to the sane and sound reasonings of the veteran
leaders; while the Slovaks, if inclined to compromise, would try
to appease the Magyars,[3] for whom Great-Austrian enthusiasms

---

[1] In the struggle which ensued there was burning of villages and mass
massacres, and atrocities were committed of an ultra-modern type: 'The
Magyars hanged prisoners of war, and the Serbs beheaded them, the
Magyars impaled their enemies and the Serbs roasted them alive, the Magyars blinded spies, and the Serbs cut out their tongues . . .' (see Springer,
op. cit., vol. ii, p. 484). Kossuth planned a complete extermination of the
Serbs in the Voyvodina—see Görgey, *Mein Leben und Wirken in Ungarn* (1852),
vol. ii, p. 104; and he ordered savage measures even against the Tran-
sylvanian Saxons—see A. Makray, *Briefe Ludwig Kossuths an F-M-L. Bem,
1849, März bis Juni* (1870), p. 2.

[2] See Wisłocki, op. cit., p. 79.

[3] For Hodža on Slovak-Magyar reconciliation, see Prelog, op. cit., p. 384.

would have been the worst provocation. But most Slovaks at
the Congress were Radicals. When a Czech spoke of the need
to preserve Austria, Štur replied:

> Our aim is to preserve ourselves. . . . Austria existed, and we were
> perishing. What would the world say if our highest aim was to save
> Austria? Her downfall is not our downfall. . . . Our chief task is to
> destroy Magyar predominance. Let us not say that we want to pre-
> serve Austria but that we want to create an Austro-Slav Empire.

And Hurban: 'We have nobler work in mind. Ignoble memories
are connected with the name of Austria.' 'It would be ridiculous
for us to want to preserve the Austrian Empire: we would have
to go against the Italians, the Poles, and perhaps against ourselves.'[1] Even Havliček, in the elation of the Congress, took a
more Radical line than before or after:

> What matters is reality. Legality will not get us far. No one at
> present works within the framework of legality. There are now
> dominant and subject nationalities in Austria. It would be easy to
> remain under Austria and attain unity, if we had the power. But for
> that the Magyars would have to be defeated.

Finally, Šafařik moved and carried a compromise resolution in
favour of 'an alliance [of the Slavs] in defence of nationality . . .
where such rights are enjoyed, and for conquering them, where
they are not'. Nothing was said either about preserving Austria,
or about revolutionary action.

In this atmosphere of growing Radicalism Libelt pulled off a
coup which altered the character of the Congress: without consulting his own Section, of which he was chairman, he carried
in an inner caucus of Congress a change of programme. How
he achieved it, is not, and perhaps never will be, known. The
Congress, instead of answering the five questions of the Organizing Committee, which had provided an Austro-Slav frame for
its work, was to issue a 'Manifesto to the Nations of Europe',
submit a Memorandum to the Emperor, and draw up a scheme
for a Slav Alliance. The Manifesto would clearly transcend the
limits originally set to the Congress and give room for raising the
Polish question in its widest international aspects. When on the
morning of 6 June Libelt reported the change to his Section, its
representatives on the drafting Committee were already chosen
(no one knows by whom),[2] and the outlines of the Manifesto

[1] Prelog, op. cit., pp. 358–62.
[2] The Polish representatives on the Committee for drafting the Manifesto
were Libelt and Moraczewski, both from Posnania, and L. Siemieński, a
Russian Pole resident in Galicia. The members who were to draft the

were prepared. The debate which ensued proved Libelt's foresight in acting in this wholly irregular manner: the genuine Ruthenes passionately opposed adopting in an appeal to Europe the customary formulation of the Polish problem which would assign them once more to the Poles, while the Poles themselves, who might have been expected to rejoice over Libelt's success, started once more raising fine points and arguing about procedure; and were still doing so when the Czechs had already finished discussing both the Manifesto[1] and the Address to the Emperor. Finally an agreement was reached between the Ruthenes and Poles through Czech mediation. The Ruthenes desisted from opposing the Poles over the Manifesto, the Poles accepted a most liberal programme securing real equality of rights for the Ruthenes in Galicia, while the question of dividing the province in accordance with nationality was referred to its future Constituent Diet. Had the Poles been sincere regarding the Agreement, the bargain would not have been disadvantageous to the Ruthenes: reforms in Galicia were capable of immediate realization, whereas the Polish postulates involved a remapping of Europe. But neither during the fifty years of Austro-Polish rule in Galicia, nor during the twenty years of its inclusion in Poland between the World Wars, did the Poles show much willingness to honour their Prague promises.[2]

Address to the Emperor had all to be Austrian subjects, and Prince Lubomirski, Prince Sapieha, and Helcel were chosen: again there was no genuine Ruthene on it, but Lubomirski sincerely favoured decent treatment of the Ruthenes, Sapieha was the most honest of the pseudo-Ruthenes, and Helcel was a Conservative. On the Committee which was to plan the Slav Alliance, Section II was represented by Cybulski and Janiszewski, two Posnanians of good intellectual calibre, and the Russian revolutionary Bakunin. Those who had planned the Congress as one of Austrian Slavs might well rub their eyes or wring their hands.

[1] In the Czechoslovak Section Vocel and Hanka objected to paragraph 4 in Libelt's draft which demanded the reunion of the divided Slav nations. Šafařik, realizing the paramount importance which the Poles attached to it, secured its acceptance in a modified form; see Odložilik, 'Slovanský sjezd a svatodušní bouře v r. 1848', in the *Slovanský Přehled*, vol. xx, pp. 408–25.

[2] With insight and foresight, Lubomirski wrote on 30 June 1848: '. . . who knows whether, if we had a government of our own it would not follow the example of the Hungarian Government which aims at a forcible Magyarization of 8 million non-Magyars'; see W. R. Wisłocki, *Jerzy Lubomirski, 1817–1872* (1928), p. 90.—Palacký tried to appease the Poles: his two schemes for a reconstruction of Austria, drawn up in the autumn of 1848 and in January 1849, make no provision for Ruthene self-government. Ziemiałkowski asserts that in the Constitutional Committee at Kremsier, the three Czech representatives, Palacký, Rieger, and Pinkas, proposed the separation of the

The Manifesto, as finally voted by the Congress, was an exceedingly vague, verbose, and ineffective document. It talks about 'our beautiful language spoken by 80 million co-racials' (just the tie which was missing), extols the virtues of the Slavs, and after referring to demands previously made for a reconstruction of Austria as a Federation of Co-Equal Peoples, protests against the Partitions of Poland (but passes over in silence the very existence of Ruthenes) and against the new partitions of Posnania; demands from the Prussian and Saxon Governments that they should cease denationalizing the Slavs in Silesia, Posnania, East and West Prussia, and Lusatia; calls on the Hungarian Government to stop violent measures against the Slavs, and to acknowledge their national rights; and demands in vague terms an improvement in the condition of the Slavs in Turkey. Lastly, the Manifesto suggests a Universal Congress of European Nations to settle all outstanding international problems. It concludes with the formula: 'In the name of the Liberty, Equality, and Fraternity of European nations.'

The Address to the Emperor was completed, but not formally adopted, before the Congress was broken up by the Whitsun riots. It sets out the demands of the Slav provinces and nationalities. Bohemia gives thanks for the Patent of 8 April, Moravia asks for similar rights and an inter-provincial connexion with Bohemia. Silesia is not mentioned: for the Teschen conflict between the Czechs and Poles had already started. Galicia asks for the rights accorded to Bohemia: a responsible Provincial Government and a Diet to draw up its constitution before the meeting of the Vienna Parliament; and the terms of the Polish Ruthene agreement are cited. The Slovaks and the Ruthenes (of Carpatho-Russia) ask for national recognition, equal representation in the Hungarian Parliament, and for permanent National Committees to watch over their interests: 'no nation shall be deemed dominant in Hungary, but all shall enjoy full rights.' The Serbs demand a union of all Serb territories of Hungary, and the Croats that of the Triune Kingdom and recognition of the acts of the Banus and Diet; the Slovenes, a union of all Slovene territories of Austria into a single province. Lastly, the Bohemians, Moravians, and Slovenes protest against

Ruthene from the Polish parts of Galicia (op. cit., part i, p. 12). This is wrong: when the vote was taken Palacký and Rieger abstained, and only Pinkas voted with Jachimowicz, the Uniat Bishop of Przemyśl, and Ratz of Vorarlberg (see Springer, *Protokolle*, p. 45).

inclusion in the new Germany, which would infringe the sovereignty of the Austrian Monarchy and subject them to a foreign Parliament. 'All Slav nations represented at the Congress unanimously support this reservation.'

The third document, 'The Act of Union between the Austrian Slavs', which was to have been submitted to the Diets of the Slav provinces, was completed by the Drafting Committee on 12 June: Austria has proclaimed equality of all her nationalities, but is drifting into dependence on the German Confederation. The Austrian Slavs conclude (without the nations now partitioned renouncing national reunion) a Slav Union which is to secure their national rights and territories, their constitutional freedoms, and the complete independence of the Austrian Empire—the Union remains under the House of Habsburg-Lorraine who must not, however, be subject to any foreign Power (i.e. must not acknowledge the supremacy of the new Germany). A Central Council of the Federated Nations is to be formed, and to meet in turn in their various capitals. The Magyars may be admitted to the Union provided they sincerely concede equality of rights to their Slavs; and the Germans, provided they shut out all supremacy of the German Confederation from their territory. Before this draft could be discussed either by the General Committee of the Congress, or the Sections, fighting in the streets of Prague put an end to their work: the Whitsun riots, although they had the Slav Congress for background, were in reality part of the general European movement, and an echo of recent events in Vienna.

There the revolutionary movement had reached its high-water mark. On 5 May under pressure of the Vienna mob, Count Ficquelmont resigned the Foreign Office; on the 15th the Government was forced to rescind the Constitution of 25 April and to agree to a Constituent Assembly elected by universal suffrage; on the 17th the Imperial Court fled to Innsbruck; and on the 26th the Committee of Public Safety was set up in Vienna, a revolutionary quasi-Government. Leo Thun, Governor of Bohemia, and Prince Alfred Windischgrätz, G.O.C. Prague, at first saw in the Czech movement a welcome counterweight to revolutionary, German-nationalist Vienna: on 17 May Thun summoned the Bohemian Diet to meet in June, and on the 29th refused to accept any further orders from the Vienna Government (whom he considered captives or accomplices of the revolutionaries); and he set up a Provisional Council in Prague consisting of the Czech leaders, Palacký, Rieger,

Brauner, and Strobach, two Bohemian noblemen, and two Germans. Had Palacký been able to retain control of the Czech movement, the programme of Czech autonomy might have been realized in an understanding with the Bohemian aristocracy and the Imperial Court. But the younger generation, especially the Prague students and artisans, were carried away by the current of European revolution, naively fraternized with the German radicals, and tried to emulate Vienna. The Congress which for a while made Prague the centre of the Western Slav world, with its festivities, demonstrations, and speeches stimulated the radical movement; in an atmosphere of excitement, which had its counterpart of apprehension and suspicion in Conservative and official circles, any trifling incident was apt to produce an explosion; especially as Windischgrätz had been waiting, ever since 13 March, for an opportunity to deal firmly with 'revolution'. On Whit Monday, 12 June, a religious service was celebrated in St. Wenceslas Square; it was followed by a demonstration, noisy but unarmed; the military attacked, and the sequel conformed to the pattern of 1848—barricades, demands for arms, for a withdrawal of the troops, &c. The moderate Czech leaders, official delegates from Vienna, and Thun himself tried to mediate, but exaltation on the one side and the wish for a show-down on the other, defeated such endeavours. The rising was insignificant as far as numbers and armament were concerned, but the military let it develop in order to crush it more effectively: on 15 June Windischgrätz withdrew his troops from Prague, and on the 17th bombarded the defenceless city. A few members of the Slav Congress were arrested, others were expelled from Prague, and an end was put to its deliberations. The actual incidents of those days are obscure and unimportant, but the after-effects were far-reaching.

'I know of no other event in our time which had more fateful consequences for our nation than the Whitsun riots', writes Palacký.[1] Martial law was proclaimed in Bohemia, the elections to the Diet were postponed, and Czech constitutional development was cut short. Had any extraneous factors contributed to the outbreak? Magyar *agents provocateurs* had undoubtedly been at work—such as the Slovak Turanský, who subsequently, as a witness before the Committee of Inquiry, told the most fanciful lies about the Congress and its origin. Conservative and official circles blamed the ubiquitous 'Polish revolutionary

[1] See *Politisches Vermächtniss* (1872), Appendix.

agents'. 'Such conduct is always expected from the Poles', wrote Bakunin in 1849, and people, acknowledging 'some kind of right in the Poles to appear whenever disturbances occur', incline to ascribe to them even 'things in which they had no share'.[1] But the German Liberals, friendly to the Poles and to 'revolution', made a more startling discovery: the riots were a Czech plot to massacre the Bohemian Germans.

In reality, there is no evidence of a single anti-German incident having occurred during the Prague riots. Helfert, himself a Bohemian German but a Conservative, wrote in the *Prager Zeitung* of 4 July 1848, that Czechs and Germans had stood together on the barricades.[2] The 'Proclamation of the Insurgents to the Inhabitants of Prague', published on 15 June after the troops had been withdrawn, thus exhorts to further action: 'The eyes of the whole of Bohemia and Moravia, of Vienna, nay of all Europe, are upon us. . . .'[3]—surely they would not have basked in Vienna's gaze had they been about to stage a massacre of the Bohemian Germans. Windischgrätz himself publicly declared on 19 June 1848, that the Prague riots were not a conflict between the two races, but an overt attack against the authority of the State.[4] Leo Thun, when asked by the Prime Minister, Pillersdorf, whether the riots had been accidental or planned, directed against specific measures and persons or of a national character, and whether the Czech National Council

---

[1] See V. Čejchan, *Bakunin v Čechach* (1928), p. 102. It was the Minutes of the Polish-Ruthene Section that the Austrian police were most anxious to find, obviously hoping to discover in them evidence of a revolutionary plot (see O. Odložilik, op. cit.); when published by Wisłocki they proved completely harmless. For stories about Polish plotters, which abound in contemporary literature, see, for instance, Comte F. de Sonis, *Lettres du Comte et de la Comtesse de Ficquelmont à la Comtesse Tiesenhausen* (1911), p. 175, and Helfert, *Aufzeichnungen und Erinnerungen aus jungen Jahren* (1904), pp. 5–6. The tale of Polish complicity was rehashed even some fifty years later by Řezniček in his book *František Palacký* (1897), pp. 180–5.

[2] See *Aufzeichnungen*, p. 4. His book, *Der Prager Juni-Aufstand 1848* (1897) and his monograph on Count Leo Thun, published in the *Oesterreichisches Jahrbuch* for 1891–5, are not in the British Museum; nor is the most recent monograph on the riots by K. Kazbunda.

[3] See * * * *r, *Alfred Fürst zu Windischgrätz* (1848), Appendix A. The author, an apologist for Windischgrätz, speaks of 'the anti-German hatred long nurtured by the ultra-Czech party'; but all he is able to say about it in a footnote, which tries to explain away things pointing in the opposite direction, is: 'As only Czech ultras stood at the head of the movement, in case of victory the struggle would certainly have assumed a national character' (p. 16).

[4] See Springer, *Geschichte Oesterreichs*, vol. ii, p. 348.

or the Slav Congress were in any way implicated, replied on 29 June:

The disturbances were not caused by national hatreds and the rising· is not to be looked upon as a fight of Czechs against Germans, but much rather as a revolt of all the radical elements against the Government, in which political passions, such as national hatreds or hostility to the nobility and the administration, were contributory factors. . . . The Slav Congress itself pursued no illegal aims, and I am convinced even now that its Czech leaders did not plan anything contrary to the law or incompatible with the interests of the Austrian Monarchy. But the revolutionary Poles and other fanatics used this welcome opportunity to come here and plot with the local revolutionary elements.[1]

But on the periphery of Bohemia, for instance at Aussig-on-Elbe, the ancestors of the modern Sudetens 'in company with Saxons and other Germans from the *Reich* joyfully celebrated the calamity which had befallen Prague, and extolled Windischgrätz as the saviour of the Germans'.[2] And a German-Bohemian historian naively observes: 'It is remarkable that outside Prague, in northern Bohemia, and still more beyond the frontiers of Bohemia, the position of its Germans should have been considered to be fraught with dangers of which they themselves had not the remotest idea.'[3]

XXI

At Frankfort German hostility to the Czechs burst forth over their refusal to be included in the new Germany, and over the Prague riots. The Germans demanded that elections for the Frankfort Parliament be held throughout western Austria, as decreed by the Pre-Parliament and the Federal Diet; the Czech National Council unanimously reserved the decision regarding the Lands of the Bohemian Crown to their own future Diet; and the Vienna Government, pitched into from both sides, finished by leaving to the constituencies themselves whether they wished to be represented at Frankfort! It would not obstruct an order of the Federal Diet, 'a legally acknowledged authority', nor interfere with 'the right of the individual citizen to participate in the work of the Frankfort Parliament', but Acts of that Parliament, to be binding in Austria, would, it declared, require its approval: thus, participation in the German National Assembly was made 'optional' and inconclusive.

[1] See Odložilik, op. cit., p. 410.   [2] See Helfert, op. cit., p. 3.
[3] See O. Weber, 'Die Prager Revolution von 1848 und das Frankfurter Parlament' in the *Festschrift des Vereines für Geschichte der Deutschen in Böhmen* (1902), p. 171.

On 25 April the Committee of Fifty dispatched from Frankfort two of its members, von Wächter, a prominent Württemberger, and Kuranda, a Bohemian Jew, to persuade the Czechs; in Prague they were joined by Schilling, a Salzburg Radical. The atmosphere was tense, and finding that the Czech National Committee had sent delegates to Vienna to secure a prohibition of elections to the Frankfort Parliament, they confined themselves to a private meeting with its Committee for Foreign Affairs. The Czechs made a show of filial solicitude for Austria —she must 'renounce none of her sovereign rights, nor would the Slavs submit to Germany', for this would destroy Austria; the Germans replied with a display of brotherly love for the Czechs—'I said', reported Wächter to the Committee of Fifty on 3 May, 'that we want to take you Bohemians into our arms— "Yes", they exclaimed, "and strangle us".' Then Schilling intervened, called freedom a specifically German achievement, and threatened the Czechs with the sharp German sword should they refuse to join Germany.[1] Having heard the reports the Committee of Fifty issued, on 5 May, a proclamation addressing 'the inhabitants of Bohemia, Moravia, and Silesia' as 'Brethren and Allies', and promising them 'in the future free and rejuvenated Germany', all the blessings which it is customary for modern whales to offer to Jonah. Elections in Bohemia, when attempted, proved a failure: only in 13 of 68 constituencies were they properly carried through, and in seven partially.

On 5 June attention was called in the Frankfort Parliament to 'the determined resistance' to elections offered in Bohemia (so far only seven members had entered the Assembly, and some of the others had resigned their seats), and a resolution was moved for a Committee to inquire into the matter, and to suggest measures which would give weight (*Nachdruck verschaffen*) to 'the will of the nation'. The tone of the debate was stridently aggressive—there was none of the sentiment which at first mellowed the debates on Poland. The much revered E. M. Arndt[2] raised a warning voice, quoting Klopstock: 'Germans, be not too just!' For where would they be if they let 'every particle' claim a national life of its own? 'We must adhere to

---

[1] Herzen writes: 'All German revolutionaries are great cosmopolitans, *sie haben überwunden den Standpunkt der Nationalität*, and are all filled with the most irritable and persistent patriotism. They are prepared to accept an all-world republic, to obliterate the frontiers between States, but Trieste and Danzig must belong to Germany'; *Byloye i dumy, Polnoye Sobranye (Collected Works)* (1919), vol. xiii, p. 352.   [2] See above, p. 84, n. 1.

the principle that what has been ours for a thousand years . . . must remain ours . . . we must protect those Germans even if greatly outnumbered by the Czechs; and deputies from Bohemia, however few, must be deemed fully to represent the country.' Schilling repeated that Germany must prevent, if necessary by the sword, a separation of Bohemia and the rise of a Slav Austria, which cannot be free 'in the German sense'. Another member protested that not a clod of German soil must be surrendered—'let the Czechs come here, and they will be welcome; if they refuse, they will still be bound by our decisions'. Hartmann (from Leitmeritz in Bohemia) thought declarations useless while the Assembly lacked executive power, but 'once we have shown our power in Holstein, we shall be able to tackle Bohemia'.

The Prague riots gave a new impulse to the anti-Czech campaign. On 20 June, Schmerling, representative of the Austrian Government in the Federal Diet, described the riots as an attack of Czechs against Germans rather than against the Government—without instructions from Vienna, but conscious of his 'sacred duty', he begged the Governments of Prussia, Saxony, and Bavaria to help, if need be, in restoring order in Bohemia, and in protecting the 'lives and property of its Germans': it was resolved to instruct them 'to hold substantial military forces in readiness' for that purpose. When the matter was reported in the Assembly, Vienna Radicals vied with members from western and northern Germany in urging immediate action. 'We do not want to wait till help is summoned', ranted Berger, a member of the Extreme Left (and 1867–70 a Minister in the Austrian Liberal Government), 'it may not be desired though necessary. It is obvious that a general massacre of Germans by the Czechs is intended.' Deetz (Wittenberg): 'Federal troops should immediately enter Bohemia . . . they will make war with vigour, as befits German troops.' And Jordan (Berlin), who five weeks later was to achieve fame through his speech on Posnania, made now a contribution no less remarkable but much less noted:

For the first time [he said] my heart swells with pride. . . . I am proud of the tremendous unanimity which at last has seized us in such a matter. I conclude that we are leaving at last the misty summits of cosmopolitanism from which one's own Fatherland is no longer visible. I see that at last we mean to proceed against the attempts of puny nationalities (*Nationalitätchen*) to found their own lives in our midst, and like parasites to destroy ours. . . .

Vogt (Giessen), a Radical, deplored that the German cause should have the reactionary Windischgrätz for its champion, but urged immediate action—or else, 'before help is summoned, the Bohemian Germans will be semi-Czechised (*so halb und halb geczecht*).' Berger and Schilling moved a resolution, complete with 'blood-bath' and 'national annihilation':

> In view of the bloody struggle which has broken out between the Czech party and the Germans in Bohemia, and the great danger of a general blood-bath and a combat of national annihilation which may ensue unless Slav fanaticism in Bohemia is checked with vigour: the German National Assembly is asked, in order to protect the Germans in Bohemia, to resolve . . . without referring the matter to a Committee, that the Federal Council should be asked . . . to order Bavarian and Saxon troops to march into Bohemia.

Thus the Czechs were not even treated as a nation in that 'war of national annihilation', but as a 'party', and the Germans were described no longer as 'in danger' but as actually engaged in a 'bloody struggle'. Venedey pleaded for some moderation towards the Czechs; war against them was 'civil war', and while many of them were unwilling to fight against the Germans, they might if violence was used; a distinction should be made between those under arms and the others.

Then came the anti-climax; three members—from Moravia, Bohemia, and Prussian Silesia—obviously better informed and realizing the nonsensical character of the debate, proceeded to reassure the House. Beidtel (Brno) argued that there was no need for outside intervention—'all superiority is with the Germans. . . . I truly believe Austria is sufficiently powerful to suppress this movement . . . it can be left to the Austrian Government to master its Slavs. Only if they fail, should we help.' And Kuranda: 'The proposal to send German troops immediately to succour the Germans, without asking the Austrian Government, would be most dangerous for the Germans.' The rural districts are quiet, and even in Prague only 'the fanatical party of the National Guard' is active. As Windischgrätz stands by the Germans 'there is no need to send troops, and I am absolutely convinced that the struggle will be over before they arrive'. But Saxony and Bavaria should be instructed to hold themselves in readiness. Lastly, Prince Lichnowsky argued that neither Austria nor Windischgrätz were likely to wish for such support, 'I therefore fail to see why we should order German federal troops from all sides to march into Bohemia—to the great amazement of its Germans.' The

Assembly decided to refer the question to the Committee for
Slav Affairs.[1]

The Committee reported on 1 July both on elections in the
Slav provinces and the position of the Germans in Bohemia:
Pan-Slavism has recently found in Prague its centre for western
Europe; it aims at uniting the Slavs of south-eastern Europe, at
dominating Austria, and engulfing its Germans and the Magyars; the Austrian Government has pursued a miserable policy
and favoured the movement in the interest of autocracy, till the
'Czech party', greatly overrating its own strength and importance,
engaged with foolish arrogance (*Uebermut*) in 'terroristic oppression of the German population'. 'The refusal to send members
to the National Assembly . . . is a direct challenge to the territorial integrity of Germany'; but Acts of the Assembly are binding even if those countries are incompletely represented.[2] Armed
intervention in Bohemia, if rashly undertaken, might have rendered general the conflict, which was limited to Prague; moreover, unsolicited help would have injured the prestige of the
Austrian Government: but the Bohemian Germans should be
assured of the help of the National Assembly, if required. The
Committee submitted resolutions calling on the Austrian Government to secure elections in the German-Slav provinces and the
attendance of their members in Parliament (or else to order by-
elections), and assuring it of most vigorous support 'in all its
measures for protecting the Bohemian Germans against attacks
by the Czech party'.

In the debate Kuranda engaged in adulation of the Bohemian
Germans and disparagement of the Czechs, ridiculed the Slav
Congress, and effusively thanked Windischgrätz. Radowitz
criticized the current 'one-sided and exclusive conception of the
principle of nationality'—'as if a great nation could confine its
most vital needs, on which its existence depends, within its own
linguistic territory'. 'The Austrian Government is now master in
Prague. Next we must demand . . . that a speedy and final end

---

[1] The Committee consisted of 15 members: 1 Saxon, 1 Bavarian, 1
Austrian resident in Bavaria, and 12 Austrians—among them Schmerling,
Sommaruga, Giskra, and Berger; 7 of them represented German constituencies in the Czech provinces, and one the Gottschee, a German enclave
in Carniola.

[2] The pressure on the Austrian Government to cause elections for Frankfort
to be held in the Slav provinces was renewed in Aug.–Sept., but the total of
members returned was 20 from Bohemia, 8 from Moravia, and 6 from
Silesia; for a full list of their names and constituencies, see Maršan, *Čechove
a Němci, r. 1848 a boj o Frankfurt* (1898).

should be made of separatist fancies, and that elections to the National Assembly be enforced without delay.' Ruge, of the Extreme Left, who in the debate on Poland was to assume the part of the revolutionary conscience, spoke against taking sides sharply, but had nothing to say for the Czechs. Perhaps the star turn of the debate came from a Moravian German, Giskra, a young man of twenty-eight (subsequently a leader of the Austrian-German Liberals and Minister of the Interior, 1867–70). He harped on the anti-German character of the Czech national movement, which threatened the Germans with 'total annihilation'. Though opposed to unsolicited intervention in Bohemia, he was not convinced of the German character of the new Austrian Government. He held no brief for Windischgrätz—

But now I cannot speak against him. By crushing an anti-German movement he has rendered the German cause victorious, and I shall pay tribute to whoever labours for the German cause, even if he is otherwise hateful to me. . . .

As a Moravian German I demand . . . that the Czech movement should be completely suppressed, and annihilated for the future. . . . I want the Moravian Germans to be . . . firmly joined to our Greater Germany . . . they will be in danger should a new Czech movement arise and spread to the Moravian Slavs, and the two together attempt separation with the help of a foreign Power.

Once more the debate closed with an anti-climax: Berger, of the 'blood-bath' resolution, recounted an incident which had occurred since. The Vienna Council of Public Safety (Great-German, radical, and anti-Czech) had sent a Commission of Inquiry to Prague. There, they who in the capital had practically supplanted the Government, met with a staggering reception: they were arrested, were cursed by the Austrian soldiers as 'Vienna dogs', and when brought before Windischgrätz were told that the revolution may have been victorious 'elsewhere' but that he, the Emperor's servant, was sole master in Prague. Berger gloomily concluded: 'This is the position in Bohemia: neither the German is victorious, nor the Czech; but both face the forces of reaction, and the time may not be distant when we shall have to defend them both against a third, dangerous, power'—as if the Frankfort Parliament could have defended anyone, or itself, against anybody.

XXII

Reaction did win, and thereby saved the reputation of the German revolution of 1848 (and of some others besides). It prevented the 'revolution of the intellectuals' from consummating *la trahison des clercs.* Had not Hitler and his associates blindly accepted the legend which latter-day liberals, German and foreign, had spun round 1848, they might well have found a great deal to extol in the *deutsche Männer und Freunde* of the Frankfort Assembly. Certain contemporaries had a saner appreciation of them—thus the Russian revolutionary Alexander Herzen, wrote in his *Memoirs*:[1]

The 'fighting Convention' assembled in St. Paul's Church at Frankfort, and consisting of well-intentioned professors, doctors, theologians, pharmacists, and philologists, *sehr ausgezeichneten in ihrem Fache*, applauded the Austrian soldiers in Lombardy and curbed the Poles in Posnania. . . . The first free word uttered after centuries of silence by the representatives of Germany seeking her own emancipation, was in opposition to the oppressed and weak nationalities. This incapacity for freedom, these awkwardly revealed inclinations to retain what had been unjustly acquired, provoke irony: insolent pretensions are forgiven only when accompanied by vigorous actions, and those were lacking.

The revolution of 1848 was marked by lack of foresight and by precipitation, but in France and in Italy there was scarcely anything ridiculous about it; in Germany, everywhere except in Vienna, it had a comic character, incomparably funnier than Goethe's wretched farce, *Der Bürgergeneral.* . . .

French weaknesses and shortcomings are palliated to some extent by their light and fugitive character. In the German the same defects assume a more solid and basic character, and hence are more striking. One must see for oneself these German efforts to play *so einen burschikosen Gamin de Paris* in politics in order to appreciate them. I was always reminded of the playfulness of a cow, when that excellent and respectable animal, adorned with domestic kindliness, takes to gambolling and galloping in the meadow, and with a serious face kicks up her hind legs or gallops sideways, whipping herself with her tail.

But the domestic story of the German revolution—that playful cow—I must leave to another essay.

[1] Op. cit., vol. xiii, pp. 252–3.